Ambrose Mong Ih-Ren

The Liberal Spirit and Anti-Liberal Discourse of John Henry Newman

PETER LANG

Bern · Berlin · Bruxelles · Frankfurt am Main · New York · Oxford · Wien

Bibliographic information published by die Deutsche Nationalbibliothek
Die Deutsche Nationalbibliothek lists this publication in the Deutsche National-
bibliografie; detailed bibliographic data is available on the Internet
at ‹http://dnb.d-nb.de›.

British Library Cataloguing-in-Publication Data: A catalogue record for this book
is available from The British Library, Great Britain

Library of Congress Cataloging-in-Publication Data

Ih-Ren, Ambrose Mong
The liberal spirit and anti-liberal discourse of John Henry Newman /
Ambrose Mong Ih-Ren.
p. cm. – (European university studies. Series XXIII, Theology, ISSN 0721-3409 ;
v. 925 = Europäische Hochschulschriften. Reihe XXIII, Theologie ; Bd. 925)
Includes bibliographical references (p.   ).
ISBN 978-3-0343-1075-8
1. Newman, John Henry, 1801-1890. 2. Liberalism (Religion)–Catholic Church.
I. Title.
BX1396.2.I37 2011
230'.2092–dc23
                                     2011037667

ISSN 0721-3409
ISBN 978-3-0343-1075-8

© Peter Lang AG, International Academic Publishers, Bern 2011
Hochfeldstrasse 32, CH-3012 Bern, Switzerland
info@peterlang.com, www.peterlang.com

Printed in Switzerland

The Liberal Spirit and Anti-Liberal
Discourse of John Henry Newman

European University Studies
Europäische Hochschulschriften
Publications Universitaires Européennes

Series XXIII
Theology

Reihe XXIII   Série XXIII
Theologie
Théologie

Vol./Band 925

PETER LANG

Bern · Berlin · Bruxelles · Frankfurt am Main · New York · Oxford · Wien

In Memory of Arthur Garcia CBE

Contents

Preface IX

Foreword XI

Introduction 1

1. Liberalism as an Ideology 9

2. Biographical Sketch 29

3. A Critic of Liberalism 57

4. The Liberal Ideas of Newman 101

5. Newman's Liberalism in the Context of
    Contemporary Pluralism 131

Conclusion 167

Bibliography 181

Preface

Not many cardinals get to be declared saints, and even rarer is one who is known for his controversial ideas and interpretation of doctrinal faith both within and outside the church. But John Henry Newman (1801-1890), beatified by Pope Benedict XVI in September 2010, was no ordinary churchman. Raised an Anglican and a leading member of the Oxford Movement in his younger days, he converted to Catholicism and, through prolific writing and polemics, established an intellectual and spiritual influence far beyond the placid, pastoral domain of the Papacy.

Time has not leveled the controversy stirred by his ideas, and scholars cannot agree whether he was anti-liberal or liberal. His beatification, the last stage before he is haloed in sainthood, only raises the incendiary level of the debate between progressives hailing him as the modern-day, bold 'Lion of Judah' and conservatives who regard him as no less than the true title-holder of 'Defender of the Faith', a role which a misguided pope once conferred on Henry VIII.

This book seeks to settle the historical question of Newman as anti-liberal or liberal, and to shed theological light on his liberal spirit and anti-liberal discourse, in order to provide fresh insights into the issue of religious pluralism. This work also relates Newman's anti-liberal polemics to Pope Benedict XVI's warning against aggressive secularism.

I am indebted to Professor Lai Pan Chiu of the Chinese University of Hong Kong who first introduced me to the writings of John Henry Newman. An accomplished scholar who has taught me how to think critically, Professor Lai is a great inspiration.

Thanks also to Francis Chin, James Baxter OP, Dr Dominic Wong GBS, OBE, JP and Maria Lachmi who proofread this work, offering many practical and creative suggestions in the process. The following persons also read some of the chapters offering very valuable comments: Patricia Byrne SSC, Columba Cleary OP, Scott Steinkerchner OP, Mary Gillis and Jon Bryan. Thanks also to Emmanuel Dispo for helping to typeset the manuscript.

I am also grateful to my friends, especially Tommy Lam and Patrick Chia, fellow Dominicans, Javier Gonzalez OP (Prior Provincial), Timoteo Merino OP, David Keong Seid OP and Ángel Daniel Blázquez OP, who have supported me with their friendship and encouragement.

Special thanks also to Ms Rosanna Wong, Mr S. E. Don Baldwin Cheng, Rev Dominic Chan VG and Rev Lawrence Lee from the Hong Kong Catholic Diocese for their generosity in supporting this work.

Chapter 4 and Chapter 5 appeared in different forms as 'The Liberal Spirit of John Henry Newman' and 'Newman and the Theology of Religions' in *Ecumenical Trends*. I would like to thank the editor, Rev James Loughran SA, for permission to include this material here.

Ambrose Mong Ih-Ren
Hong Kong
Feast of S. Mariae Magdalenae

Foreword

"Liberalism" is a multivalent word being used in various ways. Some educators might strongly advocate for liberal education or liberal studies. Some politicians might treasure liberalism as the corner-stone of their political agendas, institutions or ideals. Some ethicists might criticize liberalism as an ideology threatening the values they endeavour to safeguard. Some government officials, especially some of those in Mainland China, might consider liberalism as some sort of spiritual pollution challenging the Communist regime. Some Christians might despise liberalism as a theological heresy.

John Henry Newman (1801-1890) is famous for his polemic against liberalism on the one hand and his advocacy for liberal education on the other. The obvious questions one might ask are: Is there any contradiction involved? What did he meant by "liberal" and "liberalism"? What is his basic position - liberal, anti-liberal or post-liberal, and in what sense – political, educational or theological? Ambrose Mong's book attempts to address these questions through meticulous analysis of the historical context of nineteenth century Britain and Newman's involvement of controversies related to liberalism. On top of these, this book also aims at exploring the significance of Newman's work for the contemporary world.

Since Christianity continues to struggle with the issues related to liberalism, one has to ask the question if Newman's position formed in the nineteenth century remains relevant to the contemporary post-liberal or post-modern context. Through making references to the relevant positions of Alasdair MacIntyre, Joseph Ratzinger (Pope Benedict XVI) and Gavin D'Costa, especially their struggles with liberalism, this book helps us to appreciate the theological insights, the perpetual value and contemporary relevance of Newman's work.

As a Christian theologian working in Asia, I am very grateful to Ambrose Mong's efforts. In my last fifteen years of teaching at the only government-funded university in China with a private-funded Divinity School attached to it due to the Christian background of Chung Chi College, one of the founding liberal arts colleges of the university, I have become increasingly attracted to Newman's work, especially his idea of liberal education, his theology and his response to secularization. I am particularly pleased to see that the significance of Newman for the issue of religious pluralism, which is crucial for the Christian mission in Asia, is explored in this book by a fellow theologian from Asia.

Professor Lai Pan-chiu
The Chinese University of Hong Kong

Introduction

John Henry Newman (1801-1890) has been the subject of numerous books, articles and academic theses. A leading member of the Oxford Movement, a Roman Catholic convert from Anglicanism, a cardinal and prolific writer, Newman was already a controversial figure in his time. His beatification on 19 September 2010 and eventual canonization has ignited new interests especially among Anglicans who are disenchanted with their church and contemplating conversion to Roman Catholicism. Pope Benedict XVI in his Apostolic Constitution, *Anglicanorum Coetibus*, has introduced a new church structure that will allow former Anglicans to enter into full communion with the Catholic Church while maintaining aspects of their liturgical distinctiveness and Anglican ethos. Among Catholics, there are those who look up to him as a defender of orthodoxy and also those who lionize him as a proponent of church reforms.

In this context, understanding Newman's liberal ideas and his anti-liberal polemics can scarcely be more opportune. Historically, this book attempts to settle the question of 'liberal' and 'anti-liberal'; theologically, it seeks to demonstrate how Newman's both 'liberal spirit' and 'anti-liberal polemics' can offer new insights into the issue of religious pluralism.

The issue of liberalism continues to be debated today in the public forum and universities. On the one hand, liberalism remains influential and deeply embedded in our society that takes religious pluralism, freedom, democracy, modernity and secularization for granted. On the other hand, many contemporary intellectuals launch their severe critiques on liberalism. Newman was the foremost opponent of liberalism in his own time, and the process of his canonization, which has been making significant progress in recent years, seems to imply that many Catholics may find his thought relevant to the present day context. Some contemporary thinkers have frequently written of the crisis

1

that modernity faces – relativism, utopianism, relentless pursuit of science and technology, progress for its own sake and liberalism underlying the religious pluralism in contemporary society.

This work thus attempts to analyse Newman's anti-liberal discourse and at the same time seeks to reveal his liberal spirit in other aspects of his thought. It tries to demonstrate that Newman was indeed a liberal in spite of his public protestation. Although Newman proclaimed he was battling religious liberalism all his life, his writings and private letters proved he possessed a liberal streak in his intellectual and spiritual development. We will examine Newman's perception of the danger of the liberal spirit of his time and his possession of another kind of liberal spirit that made him so original, bold and prophetic.

This is demonstrated notably in chapter 5 which discusses the liberality of Newman's thought towards non-Christian religions. In this aspect, Newman was far ahead of his times, and it is no wonder that he is considered by many as the 'invisible *peritus*' of Vatican II. In order to evaluate the significance of Newman's ideas, this work also attempts to relate his understanding of liberalism to our contemporary pluralistic society in the relevant writings of Alasdair MacIntyre, Gavin D'Costa and especially Pope Benedict XVI.

Although writings on Newman are extensive, and hailed from various perspectives, a fresh look at the issue of liberalism in relation to Newman's works may provide us with new insights on secularization and religious pluralism. As this book seeks to demonstrate, Newman's liberal spirit is still blowing in the church and he may continue to influence our religious thought even in the pluralistic societies of Asia with its vibrant and varied religious landscape. This is because he teaches that the Christian faith carries within itself the heritage of other great religions and opens it to the *Logos*. Perhaps, Newman might find Christianity more compatible with Asian cultures than with the modern relativistic and rationalistic culture which he opposed throughout his life.

As we shall see, the kind of liberalism Newman opposed was 're-ligious' liberalism or what we would call 'secularism', which in his own words would mean, 'a world simply irreligious' – a phrase taken from his sermon on 'The Infidelity of the Future'.[1] Charles Taylor describes secularism as 'the process of disenchantment' – the disappearance of the world of spirits and moral forces. A former enchanted world has now been replaced by a world in which only human thoughts and feelings that come from the mind count.[2]

Influenced by Newman, MacIntyre said that his critique of liberalism remained constant throughout his life. His opposition to the Western liberal view must be viewed against the perspective of his contention with the eighteenth century Enlightenment rationality which sought to establish universally moral principles, but failed to provide rational justification for them. MacIntyre identifies modern liberal society as an anti-traditionalist project seeking to rise above all traditions to the vantage point of universal reason. In *After Virtue*, MacIntyre argues against Enlightenment liberalism for its presumption to neutrality. In *Whose Justice? Which Rationality?*, he argues against the possibility of universal rationality and demonstrates the tradition-specific nature of moral and philosophical enquiry.[3] This comes close to Newman's understanding of religious liberalism as an anti-dogmatic attitude leading to a subjective and rationalistic approach to faith, a denial that there are objective truths to be found in religion.

MacIntyre argues that liberalism started off as 'an appeal to alleged principles of shared rationality' against the 'tyranny of tradi-

---

1   'The Infidelity of the Future', *Faith and Prejudice*,
    http://www.newmanreader.org/works/ninesermons/sermon9.html, 124-125.
    Unless stated otherwise, all quotations and paginations of Newman's works are
    taken from *Works of John Henry Newman's* website:
    http://www.newmanreader.org/.
2   Charles Taylor, *A Secular Age* (Cambridge, Massachusetts: The Belknap Press
    of Harvard University Press, 2007), 29-30. See also Edward Norman, 'Newman's Social and Political Thinking', in *Newman after a Hundred Years*, edited
    by Ian Ker and Alan G. Hill (Oxford: Clarendon Press, 1990), 153-173.
3   MacIntyre mentions about Newman's account of tradition that is developed
    successfully in *The Arians of the Fourth Century* and *An Essay on the Development of Christian Doctrine*. See *Whose Justice? Which Rationality?*, 353-354.

tion'.[4] It claimed to provide a framework in which a common set of rational principles would allow everybody to live peacefully in society. Eventually, this liberalism was transformed into a kind of official culture that sought to impose its views on society, leading to intolerance.[5] In his *Lectures on the Present Position of Catholics in England* (1851), Newman made a satirical attack on anti-Catholic prejudice and propaganda in what was supposedly an open English society. Protestants in his time considered themselves 'liberal', but were not prepared to tolerate Catholics because they were thought to be illiberal.

There is also a remarkable similarity between Gavin D'Costa's understanding of liberal modernity and Newman's view of liberalism. D'Costa believes that a pluralist position in the theology of religions is a form of modern liberal ideology that masquerades itself as a neutral and all-embracing humanism. Influenced by MacIntyre, he asserts that religious pluralism is a child of the Enlightenment. In granting equality to all religions, the Enlightenment denied all public truth to any of them. This is an echo of Newman's critique of liberalism in religion – 'the doctrine that there is no positive truth in religion, but that one creed is as good as another, and this is the teaching which is gaining substance and force daily. It is inconsistent with any recognition of any religion, as true. It teaches that all are to be tolerated, for all are matters of opinion'.[6]

D'Costa speaks about the importance of dialogue and acknowledges that Newman bears learned testimony to Christianity's ability to synthesize critically rather than to assimilate paganism uncritically. He agrees with Newman that the original integrity of pagan beliefs, practices and rites have been 'fractured and dislocated' when they are incorporated into the Christian tradition.[7] D'Costa now supports a *uni-*

---

4   Alasdair MacIntyre, *Whose Justice? Whose Rationality?* (London: Gerald Duckworth & Co., Ltd., 1988), 335.
5   Ibid., 335-336.
6   *Biglietto Speech*,
     http://www.newmanreader.org/works/addresses/file2.html#biglietto, 64.
7   See Gavin D'Costa, *Theology and Religious Pluralism* (Oxford: Basil Blackwell, 1986),123-124.

versal-access exclusivism in his theology of religions which stresses that although explicit faith and baptism are the normal route to salvation, other means like revelation in nature, following one's conscience and reason, and elements in other religions (but not through that religion *per se*) can help us get to heaven.[8] Newman believed that tradition and the role of conscience could lead us to the truth and he was aware that the truth of the Christian faith was to be sought in relation to non-Christian religions.

In a liberal society, personal freedom is of prime importance and nothing should threaten it. Revealed religion with its dogmas as objective truths appears to threaten the individual's personal freedom. Objective truth would eventually be denied so as not to constrain personal freedom. We now live in a fragmented world known as the 'post-modern', where there is no confidence in finding meaning and commitment. In such a confused and fragmented society, only the personal, subjective and relative, seem to be of value.[9] Pope Benedict XVI recognizes this problem when he describes the church as a boat tossed on the waves by ideological currents.

Benedict laments the fact that having a clear faith based on dogma is considered fundamentalism, whereas relativism – letting oneself be swept by every kind of ideology – is considered acceptable; and hence, he wrote, 'we are moving towards a dictatorship of relativism which does not recognize anything as for certain and which has as its highest goal one's own ego and one's own desires'.[10] Influenced by Newman, Benedict believes relativism is a threat because when we abandon objective truth, it is not that we believe nothing is true, but that *anything* can be true.

Passages against liberalism are found in all stages of Newman's life and they were proclaimed loud and clear. At the same time, his

---

8   Gavin D' Costa, *Christianity and World Religions* (Oxford: Wilkey-Blackwell, 2009), 29.

9   Roderick Strange, *John Henry Newman: A Mind Alive* (London: Darton, Longman and Todd Ltd., 2008), 45.

10   See 'Cardinal Ratzinger's Homily', *Vatican Radio*, http://storico.radiovaticana.org/en1/storico/2005-04/33987.html.

liberal ideas were also evident in his bold remarks on science and philosophy, biblical inspiration and history, and his campaign against the Infallibility decree proclaimed in 1870 at the First Vatican Council. Newman avoided both a dead tradition petrified in the past and a chaotic progress. Battling against a liberalism riddled with relativism with nothing permanent which could only lead to a culture of death, Newman was all for a liberalism which joined liberty with love, thus creating a culture of life.

A few weeks after Newman's elevation as a cardinal, Johann Joseph Ignaz von Döllinger, a critic of the Vatican Council, declared that Newman's works would have been on the *Index of Forbidden Books* if the Roman prelates had understood English.[11] In fact Leo XIII's words to Lord Selborne were: 'They said he was too liberal, but I had determined to honour the Church in honouring Newman. I always had a cult for him. I am proud that I was able to honour such a man'.[12]

The book is a modest attempt to cast light on this liberal aspect of Newman and his anti-liberal rhetoric, and involves examining his works and analysing a number of secondary sources from a historical perspective. In reviewing Newman's position on liberalism in Chapter 1 by various scholars, who tend to see him as either liberal or conservative, I will argue that his stand was varied and multi-dimensional because he possessed an open mind. Newman was anti-liberal only when the church and the society at large were threatened by a certain secularising spirit. My overall conclusion is that he possessed a balanced view of things.

Chapter 2 covers Newman's upbringing and the influence of Oxford, focusing on his experience at Oriel College. The Oxford Movement in which Newman played a leading role and the prevailing liberalism then is explored with a view to understanding what aspects of the 'intellectual party' Newman was rejecting.

---

11   Erik Sidenvall, After *Anti-Catholicism?* (London: T&T Clark International, 2005),109.

12   *L'Osservatore Romano* 20 May, 2009.

Chapter 3 investigates Newman's criticism of liberalism and his defence of the dogmatic principle in religion. It covers essentially the anti-liberal polemics in his works.

Chapter 4 deals with his liberal legacy to demonstrate that he had more in common with liberal Catholicism than might have been perceived.

Chapter 5 explores his understanding of Christianity, its relation to other faiths, and the issue of religious pluralism. I see this as the culmination of Newman's liberal spirit – his acknowledgement of universal revelation, the guidance of tradition and conscience, and finally, Christianity's ability to assimilate what is good from pagan religions. In view of this, I argue that Newman may perhaps be a pioneer in understanding the significance of religious plurality.

The conclusion examines echoes of Newman in Pope Benedict XVI's writings and addresses. Benedict warned us against aggressive secularism and the dictatorship of relativism in Western society. Newman had characterized this phenomenon as a 'world simply irreligious' and 'that spirit of infidelity'.

J. M. Cameron describes the imaginative and intellectual life of the nineteenth century as dreams – 'dreams referring to the past and the future'. Newman also felt the terror and ambiguities of dreams, and 'it is the impossibility of fixing and evaluating the dream-experience that gives us great difficulty in deciding just what the attitude to Liberalism of John Henry Newman was'.[13] In the *Apologia*,[14] there is a description of Newman's journey at sea where he felt violently ill and later wrote his famous poem under 'The Pillar of the Cloud' in search for direction:

> Lead, kindly Light, amid the encircling gloom,
> Lead Thou me on!
> The night is dark, and I am far from home—

---

13   J.M. Cameron, 'Newman and Liberalism', *Cross Currents* 30, no. 2 (Summer 1980), 154.

14   *Apologia pro Vita Sua*,
       http://www.newmanreader.org/works/ apologia65/index.html.

Lead Thou me on!
Keep Thou my feet; I do not ask to see
The distant scene—one step enough for me.

This book, above all, seeks to shed light on Newman's ideas of liberalism and its significance for Christianity in our secularized and pluralistic society.

Chapter 1

Liberalism as an Ideology

Liberalism in its original form is a moral and political outlook in which autonomy is of great importance; it is against constraint and coercion. For the individual, liberalism means having self-determined thought and action consistent with the principle of not harming others. True liberalism is a social contract in which the right of all individuals to pursue their own good is acknowledged. A liberal thus identifies the political good with the will of the people.[1]

There are three basic types of liberalism that have emerged over the last few centuries. Historically the first one is now known as classical liberalism or libertarianism and teaches that everyone is entitled to a general right of liberty. It insists on general liberty as the only real concern of the state, and according to John Locke, 'no one ought to harm another in his life, health, liberty or possessions'.[2] That means no one including the state can impose on anyone a line of action except to stop the person from harming others. To counter fraud or violence is the only legitimate reason for using coercion.[3]

The second type of liberalism is egalitarianism and believes that the public must impose on everyone the goal of bringing some specific form of equality. This means that we must promote the goods of individuals especially the goods of those below the median. The ideal society thus is when as much as possible everyone is well off. Egalitarianism calls for much greater intervention into the lives of people

---

1   Jan Narveson and Susan Dimock, eds., *Liberalism* (Dordrecht ; Boston : Kluwer Academic Publishers, 2000), 1.

2   Quoted in Jan Narveson and Susan Dimock, eds., *Liberalism* (Dordrecht ; Boston: Kluwer Academic Publishers, 2000), 25.

3   Ibid., 24-25.

than classical liberalism. Ironically, egalitarianism stands at the other extreme of libertarianism within the general framework of liberal philosophy.[4]

The third variety, welfare liberalism, is a synthesis between classical liberalism and egalitarianism. It proposes the state to intervene whenever there is a need to achieve a balance in the distribution of goods. This means everyone is entitled to a certain broad minimum of the basic means to live a good life. Coercion may be used to distribute resources for the general welfare of people without violating liberal principles. In this welfare liberalism, society is a kind of insurance system that ensures a minimum of health, education and income for all. All the above types of liberalism agree that public institutions are to be devoted to the good of individuals.

Liberalism as an ideology dominated the nineteenth century. It is more of a motto than a word, 'more a programme of what might be than a description of what was'.[5] Some saw it as a coherent theory while others saw it as the destruction of a stable society. After the Reformation, liberalism often meant freedom that led to immorality, licentiousness or anarchy.

At times religious people use the words 'liberal' and 'liberalism' to mean evil. In the nineteenth century some thought that liberals wanted too much freedom which would lead to wickedness and which ironically would be the end of freedom to live a good life.[6] In 1864, the church condemned the idea that it needed to reconcile to liberalism in the *Syllabus of Errors*. The liberals of the nineteenth century put freedom above all else. Modern ideas of freedom were founded in religious toleration originating from John Locke in the seventeenth century; it was based on the principle of a natural right to freedom of conscience which no government could tamper with. This natural right includes freedom of opinion and expression.[7]

---

4   Ibid., 25.
5   Owen Chadwick, *The Secularization of the European Mind in the Nineteenth Century* (Cambridge: Cambridge University Press, 1975), 21.
6   Ibid., 22.
7   Ibid., 25.

In Western Europe the claim of the liberals was religious: liberal faith rested on religious dissenter. Liberalism meant criticism of medieval religious orthodoxy. Dissenters won the freedom to express opinion contrary to orthodox belief. The right to dissenting religious opinion led to practice.[8] Freedom of religious opinion includes the right not to believe as well, and liberalism thus included the right to be secular. If there is freedom not to believe in religion, then the state cannot force individuals to be religious. Thus the liberal state logically leads to the secular state. But Owen Chadwick is quick to say that the liberalism of the nineteenth century did not always lead to secularism; it was only a tendency towards that direction.[9]

What, then, does Newman mean by Liberalism?

Obviously, Newman's understanding of liberalism does not fall neatly into any of the categories discussed. In 1841, he considered the spirit of liberalism as the characteristic of the anti-Christ. Doctrine wise, he was a conservative, but he was very much a liberal when it comes to ecclesiastical politics. The complexity of the issue of liberalism is well articulated by Chadwick: 'What Newman denounced as liberalism, no one else regarded as liberalism' and thus, he could be anti-liberal in his terms, but a liberal nonetheless.[10] Others classified him as a liberal at a time when he regarded himself as an anti-liberal. And both views could be right. Chadwick also argues that many people see Newman as illiberal simply because he kept saying so and refused to recant although some of his writings proved to be otherwise.[11] Perhaps as a young man, he was a bigot, and his views developed as he aged, but

8   Ibid., 26.
9   Ibid., 27.
10   Owen Chadwick, *Newman* (Oxford: Oxford University Press, 1983), 74.
11   Ibid.

the essential Newman, the man who fought relentlessly against the spirit of liberalism in religion remains, even though the meaning of liberalism has evolved.

Of particular interest to the intellectual community of Victorian society is Newman's position on liberalism, which seemed to vacillate depending on the issues, timing and circumstances. In public, he claimed to be an anti-liberal, as in his *biglietto* speech on May 12, 1879, on receiving the cardinal's red hat from Pope Leo XIII. But in some of his writings, he came across as a liberal who supported modernist tendencies on various issues.

The principles of the French Revolution (1789) are considered the foundation of a new form of liberalism. One of its most fundamental principles asserts an absolute and unrestrained freedom of thought, religion, conscience, creed, speech, press, and political alliance. This resulted in the abolition of every kind of authority derived from God and the withdrawal of religious practice from the public life into the private domain of one's individual conscience. Liberals took the view, as enshrined in the 1776 American Declaration of Independence that human being has certain inalienable rights, which are not subject to any 'absolute despotism'. Newman believed this view would eventually lead to the denial of all true authority including religion and God.

According to Louis Groarke, the Protestant Reformation represents a rebellion against an abusive authority, and liberalism is the emptying out of the Protestant ideal – 'a vacant Protestantism'.[12] The Reformers waged wars against what they perceived to be *false* authority. Liberalism goes one step further; it not only rejects false and abusive authority, but it rejects all authority.[13] The individual reigns supreme – it is an amoral autonomy: you are free to do as you please. Newman was aware that liberalism was the offspring of the Protestant Reformation, and secularism the grandchild.

---

12   Louis Groarke, 'What is Freedom? Why Christianity and Theoretical Liberalism Cannot Be Reconciled?', *Heythrop Journal XLVII* (2006), 262.
13   Ibid., 262-263.

The liberalism Newman experienced was essentially a product of the eighteenth century Enlightenment. By the early nineteenth century, there was not much unity among the liberals. In short, the liberals were not a uniform intellectual or political monolithic. However, they would reject the Orthodox's idea that the Church of England was the 'one visible Catholic Church' and also the claim of the Evangelicals on the 'narrow limits within which they confined the Gospel'.[14] In this regard, compared with the liberals, Newman was certainly on the side of tradition and orthodoxy. However, it must be stressed that he did not reject liberalism outright, but only certain aspects of it, particularly those that touched on religion. He shared the basic Tory conservatism of an Anglican priest, but as a son of a banker, his political and religious thoughts tend towards a more liberal posture than other conservatives.

Newman was against a liberalism that can also be classified as 'secular liberalism' – that strand of liberalism which construed individual freedom in secular terms, rooted in the moral and spiritual autonomy of the person.[15] Broadly speaking, liberalism refers to the same phenomenon as the Enlightenment, or Modernity – the attempts to achieve humanity by first domesticating, and later by rejecting and replacing Christian culture.[16] He expresses forcefully the dangers of religious liberalism in his *biglietto* speech:

Christianity has been too often in what seemed deadly peril, that we should fear for it any new trial now. So far is certain; on the other hand, what is uncertain, and in these great contests commonly is uncertain, and what is commonly a great surprise, when it is witnessed, is the particular mode by which, in the event, Providence rescues and saves His elect inheritance. Sometimes our en-

---

14   Quoted in Francis McGrath, *John Henry Newman: Universal Revelation* (Mulgrave, Victoria: John Garratt Publishing, 1977), 51.
15   Jonathan Chaplin, 'Rejecting Neutrality, Respecting Diversity: From "Liberal Pluralism" to "Christian Pluralism" ', *Christian Scholar's Revie* 35, no. 2 (January 1, 2006), 145.
16   Francisco Javier Martínez, ' "Beyond Secular Reason": Some Contemporary Challenges for the Life and Though of the Church', *Communio: International Catholic Review* 31, (Winter 2004), 558.

emy is turned into a friend; sometimes he is despoiled of that special virulence of evil which was so threatening; sometimes he falls to pieces of himself; sometimes he does just so much as is beneficial, and then is removed. Commonly the Church has nothing more to do than to go on in her own proper duties, in confidence and peace; to stand still and to see the salvation of God.[17]

Newman continues with a call to the church to halt this 'error' overspreading through the world like a 'snare'. Liberalism or secular reason has the immense ability to disguise itself, to present itself as the natural way of doing things – it is timeless and universal, so to speak. He urged church leaders to make intellectual and moral efforts to unmask its strategies, expose its ideological character and return to tradition.

And yet Newman questions and deals with theological and ecclesiastical issues. According to Terrence Kenny, it was Newman's contact with the celebrated Noetics in Oriel College 'whose readiness to question established ideas and institution that the liberal influence in question is most pronounced', that led Newman to contemplate 'the trial of some of these institutions at the bar of reason'.[18] He gradually learned to distinguish between what was important and what was not, and thus, he was more ready for change than many of his contemporaries. As an Anglican, Newman was prepared to face the disestablishment of the Church of England, and as a Catholic he desired to see the end of the pope's temporal power. This readiness to challenge and change established institutions, and status quo was a hallmark of the liberal spirit that Newman shared. He reserved his liberalism for specific cases.[19]

At Oxford, his Calvinistic Evangelical upbringing gave way to a more 'humanistic' outlook and he began to value human endeavour in thought and action. Thus, as a Catholic, he could teach about the virtues of a liberal education, leading some people to think that Newman

17   *Biglietto* Speech,
      http://www.newmanreader.org/works/addresses/file2.html#biglietto, 69-70.
18   Terrence Kenny, *The Political Thought of John Henry Newman* (London: Longman, Green and Co., 1957), 9.
19   Ibid.,10.

14

only developed his liberal attitude as a Roman Catholic, but Kenny argues it was in his younger days spent in the Oriel Common Room that Newman developed his liberal outlook. And whatever changes in Newman's political and religious beliefs took place in 1845, and the liberal influence of the Noetics remained with him throughout his life.[20] Newman was prepared for reform in established institutions, and, at the same time, he too believed in the need for continuity and organic growth – it is a question of what needs to be changed and what remains. One of his qualities was the ability to distinguish the essence from the accidental, the permanent from the temporal.

The liberalism that Newman fought against in Oxford was actually a theological party which by 1864 had spread throughout the educated laity, growing from a school to become an ideology. Adrian Hastings' view is more theological when he states that Newman's use of the word 'liberalism' has to be viewed 'within the context both of an Augustinian theology and a perception of nineteenth-century history at once pessimistic and perspicacious'.[21]

Mathew Arnold is more precise and specific when he asserts that the liberalism that Newman perceived was 'the great middle class Liberalism' which includes 'belief in the Reform Bill of 1832 and local self government, in politics'; in the social sphere, it includes 'free trade, unrestricted competition, and the making of industrial fortunes'; in the religious sphere, it includes the 'Dissidence of Dissent and the Protestantism of the Protestant religion'. He goes on to say that this impulse was opposed to the Oxford Movement in which Newman was the animating spirit, the force that was dominant in the country and that would persist in the future – 'the great force of Philistinism'.[22] In other words, Newman fought against the spirit of social, political philistinism, and the vulgar Protestantism that was current in his time. Eventually this led him to leave the church of his birth to join the Ro-

---

20   Ibid.
21   Adrian Hastings, *The Theology of a Protestant Catholic* (Philadelphia: Trinity Press International, 1990),124.
22   Quoted in Erik Sidenvall, *After Anti-Catholicism?* (London: T&T Clark International, 2005), 78.

15

man communion which could only happen without much hindrance in a liberal and open society.

John F. Crosby argues that in all its stages of development, liberalism maintains a unifying spirit which led Newman to protest it again and again for fifty years.[23]

However, Lee H. Yearley claims that Newman's writings on the subject cover fifty years and they are mostly polemical and reflect the diversity of English Liberalism. The 'Liberal Spirit' is diversified because, as Newman said, it is not just a party, but the educated secular world. Nonetheless, in general he recognised it as 'one and the same everywhere', though 'in detail and in character, it varies'.[24]

In the theological context, liberalism changed during Newman's lifetime and the nuances of his thought developed due to historical circumstances.[25] For example, after the promulgation of the *Syllabus of Errors* in 1864, liberalism included hostility to biblical and ecclesiastical orthodoxy. Thus, to both Protestants and Catholics, Newman could appear as a long time champion of religious dogmas against those who embarked on speculative study of the Bible and those who questioned church authority.

Terrence Merrigan argues that Newman's attitude towards liberalism is more nuanced; hence both liberals and conservatives can find support in his writings to justify their cause or to serve their theological agendas. He appealed to people holding different shades of theological opinion.[26] Newman's reputation as a writer and Christian was never in doubt, but the liberals could not make up their minds whether he was one of them or an enemy of modernism and progress after his secession. This is because Roman Catholicism was identified with a

---

23   John F. Crosby, 'Newman's witness against the spirit of liberalism in religion', *John Henry Newman* (Rome: Urbaniana University Press, 1981), 101.

24   Lee H. Yearley, 'Newman's concrete specification of the distinction between Christianity and liberalism', *Downside Review* 93, no. 310 (January 1975), 43.

25   J. Derek Holmes, 'J.H. Newman: History, Liberalism and the Dogmatic Principle', *Philosophical Studies* 23 (1975), 86.

26   Terrence Merrigan, 'Newman and theological liberalism', *Theological Studies* 66, no. 3 (September 2005), 605.

reactionary anti-modern force which published the infamous *Syllabus of Errors* and *Quanta Cura*. Newman's private opinion on these documents is difficult to fathom – was he a faithful champion of the Roman Catholic Church or was he in reality a covert liberal aligning himself with the British public against the Roman Curia?

Mark S. Burrows argues that Newman's anti-liberal understanding of the church has not been recognised by scholars, both Catholics and Protestants, who chose to focus on the progressive and ecumenical dimension of his thought. These scholars attempt to discover Newman through a selective reconstruction of his thought. Burrow also maintains that Newman's stress on church authority is a central concern in his Catholic writings despite his moderate position as compared to the Ultramontanes – his self-avowed anti-liberal position stand at the heart of his insistence on the church's role in scientific inquiry.[27] Burrows also maintains that there is 'no temper of liberalism', but only Newman's relentless struggle against the liberal spirit – 'the dialectic not of sin and grace, but rather reason and the Church'.[28] He claims that Newman was becoming more sceptical regarding critical scholarship and its place in the church, and that the modern 'rediscovery' of Newman as a liberal is an approach that distorts Newman's thought because he was staunchly anti-liberal, and was thoroughly against modernism.[29]

Clearly, we can find many examples of Newman's vehement anti-liberal sentiments against the Whigs in their influence on the Established Church, as he says of some unfortunate people – 'they are Liberals, and in saying this I conceive I am saying almost as bad of them as can be said of anyone'.[30] He went to the extent of calling these people 'vermin', in other words, pests or parasites. The violent

27 Mark S. Burrows, 'A historical reconsideration of Newman and liberalism, Newman and Mivart on science and the church', *Scottish Journal of Theology* 40, no. 3 (1987), 401.
28 Ibid., 418.
29 Ibid., 418-419.
30 Quoted in Terrence Kenny, *The Political Thought of John Henry Newman* (London: Longman, Green and Co., 1957), 129.

opposition is not due to any hatred of an abstract liberalism, but due to a specific situation - his fear for the safety of his church in the hands of the Whigs. [31]

His reputation as a theologian and philosopher was ambiguous, as Erik Sidenvall suggests, and the 'Janus-like qualities of his mind continues to perplex the public'.[32] There are two antagonistic accounts of Newman: on the one hand, he was a life-long anti-liberal, and on the other, he was 'a romantic ally of the liberal spirit', revealing an 'implicit liberalism', especially after he became a Catholic.[33]

The liberal temper of Newman is revealed in his *Letter to the Duke of Norfolk* when he expresses his limited view of papal infallibility in contrast to the Ultramontanists who wanted to extend papal power to both the spiritual and temporal spheres. In this letter, he affirms that the consciences of Catholics were not bound to the teaching of the pope as he writes 'I shall drink – to the Pope, if you please – still, to Conscience first, and to the Pope afterwards'.[34] By writing a reply to Gladstone who believed that Catholicism infringed civil loyalty, Newman revealed himself to be a champion of liberal-minded Catholicism.

In writing the *Apologia pro Vita Sua,* Newman was concerned with gaining public and not divine vindication, and according to Sidenvall, this shows that he was 'a representative of a decidedly 'modern' post-Rousseau attitude towards autobiographical writing'.[35] In this work, he tries to court the liberal sentiment of his countrymen, reveals himself to his readers as a man compelled to follow his conscience, and asserts that in his spiritual journey, he loves honesty bet-

31 Ibid.
32 Erik Sidenvall, *After Anti-Catholicism?* (London: T&T Clark International, 2005), 104.
33 Terrence Kenny, *The Political Thought of John Henry Newman* (London: Longman, Green and Co., 1957), 127.
34 *Letter to the Duke of Norfolk,* http://www.newmanreader.org/works/ anglicans/ volume2/ gladstone/section5.html, 261.
35 Erik Sidenvall, *After Anti-Catholicism?* (London: T&T Clark International, 2005), 85.

ter than name and truth better than friends. In the *Apologia*, Newman also recognises that the meaning of liberalism depends on time and circumstances, and thus, it is best understood as a state of mind, a fundamental attitude that may exist without the individual being aware of it.[36] Liberalism is parallel to Modernism in the Catholic sense, and as a result of this ambivalent meaning of liberalism, Newman can be said to be both the guardian of orthodoxy and the father of Modernism – we can find in his writings cogent texts to support both views.

Newman recognised the positive aspects of liberalism, even in religion as he pointed out that 'there is much in the liberalistic theory which is good and true; for example... the precepts of justice, truthfulness, sobriety, self-command, benevolence'. The problem is not so much the principle of liberalism as such, but the attempt to use this principle to obliterate religion. When this happens, liberalism becomes evil.[37] Thus, for Newman, liberalism was not evil in itself, because as a social and cultural phenomenon liberalism has many virtues especially in an age where society and the church are falling apart under the influence of rational enquiry, political efficiency and pluralism. It promotes the liberal virtues of tolerance, democracy and freedom which are essential to the preservation of society. He recognised too that there was no going back to the authoritarian and monolithic tradition of the past. For Newman, the church could not afford to oppose liberalism in the political and social spheres, but must exercise her authority reasonably and judiciously or Christianity will suffer. This is reflected in his understanding of the role of the theologian and the practice of theology.[38]

Edward Jeremy Miller asserts that Newman formed his view of the church in a highly authoritarian phase of Roman Catholicism, and although he defended Rome's authority in matters of doctrine, in many ways his full views were different from the mentality of the

---

36   Terrence Merrigan, 'Newman and theological liberalism', *Theological Studies* 66, no. 3 (September 2005), 607.

37   Ibid., 610.

38   Ibid.

age.[39] In other words, he was a liberal who fought for an open church, against the Ultramontanists and their backers. Although the title of cardinal seemed to have restrained him somewhat, Newman was 'the great polemist against church detractors' and champion of laity's rights. He advocated freedom of thought, and as a critic of authoritarianism of the church, he fought for more freedom in the church for three decades. Newman was able to integrate his love for the church and to criticise its defects: he was both loyal and questioning.[40]

A man not unaccustomed to controversy, Newman was constantly dealing with misunderstandings and suspicions. Although he had been converted to Roman Catholicism which he believed was the true church, he did not think it was perfect, and he advocated reforms in ecclesiastical authority and theological reflection which were over-centralized. Newman was against clericalism that paid little attention to the life of the laity.

As a result of these efforts, he met suspicions and objections from church authorities. At the same time, his Anglican friends and foes thought his conversion was insincere and speculated on his return to the Church of England after he realised that he had made a mistake. But Newman's conversion was firm, and because he loved his new spiritual home, he could not remain silent about the need for reforms in the Catholic Church. As a public figure whatever position he took would be widely reported and hence, he experienced the great tension of being a committed Catholic and a reforming voice. Miller maintains that it is in Newman's private correspondence that he tried to deal with this conflict, and his theology reveals tensions and polarities.[41]

A champion of freedom of thought in theological reflection, Newman also recognised the legitimate claims of the Magisterium authority in monitoring the works of theologians. He supported the laity, and yet the laity and theologians had limits to which they were

---

39   Edward Jeremy Miller, *John Henry Newman on the Idea of Church* (West Virginia: The Patmos Press, 1987), xvi.
40   Ibid., xvii.
41   Ibid., xviii.

accountable. Concern with how church teaching came about and how it was assimilated, Newman wrote about the *sensus fidelium* (the consultation process) and *consensus fidelium* (the reception process).

Newman maintained great respect for authority, but at the same time he was moving against the leadership of the Catholic Church under Pius IX with his reforming voice. As a result, English Catholics, from the 1860s onwards, who valued freedom of opinion and open discussion, looked to Newman for direction, and in this he managed to provoke the ecclesiastical authority. Considered an ally by some Catholics who were dissatisfied with papal policy, he was an icon for the reform-minded Catholics in the early twentieth century. If not for its counterproductive aspects, Newman would have supported the authority of the pope in the modern world and also papal authority exercised in an authoritarian manner. Eventually, for practical purposes, he concealed his conservative view of the role the church ought to play in the public life of the nation and his later Catholic period was characterised by a 'preference for the tolerant and even neutral state'.[42]

Paul Misner argues that Newman, given his conservative stance, could still be considered a 'Liberal Catholic' although he might not qualify based on Acton's definition that Liberal Catholics are those who wanted freedom for the church and in the church.[43] He was a Liberal Catholic in the sense that he preferred, out of concern for the faith, open discussion of issues and doctrines. Newman deplored authoritarianism which used censorship to suppress freedom and what he called 'narrowing the lines of communion'.[44] He was for open rather than authoritarian approaches in church's dealings with his contemporary society. The epithet 'liberal' is ambiguous and creates confusion, and Misner argues that Newman took a cautious line by using it primarily in a pejorative sense, focussing on its tendency to relativize in religious matters. In the 1865 edition of the *Apologia* Newman added a 'Note' on 'Liberalism' to explain his usage of the word in the con-

---

42 Paul Misner, 'The "liberal" legacy of John Henry Newman', *Newman and the Modernists* (Lanham, Md: University Press of America, 1985), 5.
43 Ibid.
44 Ibid., 6.

text of Oxford in the 1830s. People in England had generally come to associate 'liberal' with democratic principles and political reform of the kind promoted by the Liberal Party.[45]

Cameron claims that Newman's liberal ideas are found in his notebooks not intended for publication.[46] Jan Walgrave argues that Newman's psychological attitude towards close friends was very different from his attitude towards the general public to whom he addressed himself in his discourses and his many controversial writings. To the public and anonymous circle of hearers and readers, Newman skilfully adapted and reserved his ideas with 'economical limitation and rhetorical fitness', but to his close friends, he felt greater freedom to express his convictions and opinions without restraint.[47] He possessed a liberal spirit in many aspects, though at times he engaged in anti-liberal rhetoric.

Newman was an influential figure and he never failed to adapt and limit his ideas and counsels to the needs and capacities of his audience. Some of his letters are 'masterpieces of cunning circumspection and subtle irony'.[48] But with his friends, relatives and family members, he was 'easy, tender, pleasant, and openhearted', which can be seen in his private correspondence.[49] Hence, one discovers 'unaccustomed candour' in his correspondence as Newman could express himself bluntly and unguardedly especially when he criticized the misuse of authority in the church and deplored the treatment of individuals.[50]

There was also a time when Newman had to keep silent for a political reason. His letters before and during the writing of *An Essay in Aid of a Grammar of Assent* (1870) reveal that he was anxious not to

45   Ibid., 10-11.
46   J.M. Cameron, 'Newman and Liberalism', *Cross Currents* 30, no. 2 (Summer 1980), 155.
47   J.H. Walgrave's Foreword in Edward Jeremy Miller, *John Henry Newman on the Idea Of Church* (West Virginia: The Patmos Press, 1987), ix.
48   Ibid.
49   Ibid.
50   Ibid., xxi.

provoke the Sacred Congregation of Propaganda in Rome which he once referred to as a 'quasi-military power'.[51] The *Rambler* affair of 1859 had raised doubts about his theological soundness and so he chose to remain silent.[52] This was the time he was afraid of putting his ideas on paper, for he thought that 'this age of the Church is peculiar – in former times, primitive and medieval, there was not the extreme centralisation which now is in use'.[53] In those days 'the Holy See was but the court of ultimate appeal. Now, if I, as a private priest, put anything into print, *Propaganda* answers me at once. How can I fight with such a chain on my arm? It is like the Persians driven on to fight *under the lash'*.[54]

Although Newman considered a particular form of liberalism an infection or pollution, his acquaintance with French liberals like Lacordaire taught him to take the political situations and traditions as they were and to make the best of them.[55] In fact, as Hastings points out, by the 1860s, Newman accepted the fact that the liberal society had come to stay, and 'his political anti-liberal phobia had almost completely disappeared: it might remain as a verbal whimsy but in practical politics he now normally preferred the liberal option'.[56] In 1879, he said that in a democratic and religiously pluralistic society,

51 Quoted in Francis McGrath, *John Henry Newman: Universal Revelation* (Mulgrave, Victoria: John Garratt Publishing, 1977), 89.

52 Francis McGrath, *John Henry Newman: Universal Revelation* (Mulgrave, Victoria: John Garratt Publishing, 1977), 89. For an account of the *Rambler* affair, see Ian Ker's *John Henry Newman* (Oxford: Oxford University Press, 1988), 463-489.

53 Quoted in Francis McGrath, *John Henry Newman: Universal Revelation* (Mulgrave, Victoria: John Garratt Publishing, 1977), 89.

54 Ibid.

55 J.M. Cameron, 'Newman and Liberalism', *Cross Currents* 30, no. 2 (Summer 1980), 155-156.

56 Adrian Hastings, *The Theology of a Protestant Catholic* (Philadelphia: Trinity Press International, 1990), 123.

'the liberal principle is forced on us from the necessity of the case ... We cannot help ourselves'.[57]

Cameron also suggests that Newman's ambivalent attitude towards liberalism was due to his 'reflexivity' and he thought of himself and others as 'single inhabitants of an epistemological solitude'.[58] According to him, '... [Newman's] combination of a firm attachment to dogmatic principles with an awareness of the logical and epistemological difficulties attaching to their statement and reception by the faithful in part explains, as do his peculiarities of temperament and psychic structure, his ambivalent attitude to Liberalism'.[59]

If his sharpest observations are found in his notes not intended for public consumption, as Cameron claims, could it be that Newman tried to portray himself as an anti-liberal in public, but in private, he was a die-hard liberal at heart?

Newman believes that even heresies bear a grain of truth. It becomes heresy when the grain is taken for the only truth – 'Mistakes carry information for they are cognate to the truth', according to Newman.[60] He writes:

Nay, the doctrines even of the heretical bodies are indices and anticipations of the mind of the Church. As the first step in settling a question of doctrine is to raise and debate it, so heresies in every age may be taken as the measure of the existing state of thought in the Church, and of the movement of her theology; they determine in what way the current is setting, and the rate at which it flows.[61]

Perhaps the best way to describe Newman's intellectual ability is his balanced view of things. According to Walgrave, 'Newman was very

57   *Biglietto*   *speech.*
      http://www.newmanreader.org/works/addresses/file2.html#biglietto, 67-68.
58   J.M. Cameron, 'Newman and Liberalism', *Cross Currents* 30, no. 2 (Summer 1980), 157.
59   Ibid., 165.
60   *An   Essay   on   the   Development   of   Christian   Doctrine*, http://www.newmanreader.org   /works/development/index.html, 224.
61   Ibid., 362.

gifted: he was endowed with many gifts in a very high degree and he made the best of his gifts by using them, by exercise, discipline and training. Richness and balance are the characteristics of a really great mind and Newman's many and various gifts, developed to the full were integrated into a highly balanced whole'.[62] Walgrave goes on to assert that 'in a balanced mind both opposite tendencies are united in mutual tension and conflict in such a way however that in their dialectical to and fro the one does not exclude or enfeeble, but rather allows and even enhances the full functioning of its opposite ... matter-of-factness and imagination are equally strong'.[63]

Thus we see Walgrave attempting to resolve the 'Newman riddle' by saying there are healthy 'polarities' and a consistent 'balance' in Newman's thought. Ian Ker makes the same point when he writes: 'The mind of Newman, I argue, is characterized not by contradictions but by complementary strengths, so that he may be called, without inconsistency, both conservative and liberal, progressive and traditional, cautious and radical, dogmatic yet pragmatic, idealistic but realistic'.[64]

Hastings also acknowledges this equilibrium in Newman's thought and admits that the strain of balancing between fighting the liberal spirit in religion and acknowledging the positive aspects of liberalism must have been great on such a delicate and gentle soul as Newman. He was able to maintain this balance for forty years in which he was able to pass on the benefits to a more open church because of the integrity of his faith, his far-sightedness and the profundity of his judgment.[65]

Kenny argues that Newman was a conservative in 'the deepest sense of the word', and in order to understand his liberal attitude, we

62   J.H. Walgrave, *John Henry Newman* (Rome: Urbaniana University Press, 1981), 157.
63   Ibid., 158.
64   Ian Ker , *John Henry Newman* (Oxford: Oxford University Press, 1988), viii.
65   Adrian Hastings, *The Theology of a Protestant Catholic* (Philadelphia: Trinity Press International, 1990), 132.

must take into account his basic conservatism.[66] But Newman was not a conservative in the sense that he was anxious to preserve the status quo and state of affairs – it was not a narrow self-interest nor a conviction rooted in his temperament. His conservatism lay in his profound sense of order and harmony in the universe, a general pessimism about man and his capabilities, and a great sympathy for the past. His sense of order extended throughout the visible and invisible world and included all forms of life. This profound sense of harmony led Newman to believe that even unjust law is preferable to disorder.[67]

Newman's conservatism can be traced to the Romantic revival of his age. In fact, he can be considered as one the great Romantics together with Coleridge and Scott in particular, who had aroused in Newman an interest in history. According to Kenny, 'Newman's approach was thoroughly historical, and was conservative because it was historical'. When confronted with any specific issue or problem, he strove to place it within its historical context.[68] As a Catholic, he was able to view controversial issues 'through the long vista of the centuries', and thus, he was able to take a more balanced approach in any hotly debated issue of the day.[69] Kenny also makes this insightful observation that 'if violent opposition to any form of liberalism is sufficient to make one a conservative, then Newman was a conservative indeed, and it is the tone and temper of this opposition of Newman's which has been largely responsible for the widely received picture of him as an ultra-conservative cleric'.[70]

In spite of his public opposition to religious liberalism, Newman was proclaimed to be the chief nineteenth century prophet of Liberal Catholicism and the veritable father of the Second Vatican Council – a liberal development in the church itself. Hence, the anti-liberal Englishman became the Catholic liberal. Butler says this of Newman:

66   Terrence Kenny, *The Political Thought of John Henry Newman* (London: Longman, Green and Co., 1957), 24-25.
67   Ibid., 47.
68   Ibid., 27.
69   Ibid., 28.
70   Ibid., 31.

26

'The tide has been turned, and a first, immensely important step has been taken towards the vindication of all the main theological, religious, and cultural positions of the former Fellow of Oriel'. Derek Holmes notices 'something of a liberal temper' in Newman's writings and acknowledges that he was 'the symbol of the hope of English Liberal Catholics'.[71] Newman was also a true liberal in the Aristotelian sense – among other things, he advocated the cultivation of knowledge, and the possession of truths for their own sakes without consideration for their utility, in his *The Idea of a University*.

All his life, Newman was searching for the truth which eventually led him into the Roman Catholic Church – after a thorough study of the Early Fathers and the whole history of the church. He concluded that ignorance of history usually led to Protestantism, while a knowledge of history led to Catholicism as the splendour of the truth. Thus, when Charles Kingsley wrote that 'Truth, for its own sake, had never been a virtue with the Roman clergy, Father Newman informs us that it need not, and on the whole ought not to be', Newman responded swiftly with his *Apologia*.[72] Chadwick says that it was fortunate that by 1864 Newman was not a saint, for he would not accept Kingsley's apology, but chose to whip the man on the ground by producing this literary masterpiece that made Kingsley looked small and foolish.[73]

There is enough evidence to show Newman supported some forms of liberalism: he was the champion of liberal education and opposed the narrow educational ideal of utilitarianism which was prevalent during his time. He was a liberal in the sense that he was opposed to what he believed to be the inopportune definition of papal infallibility because he was afraid that it would be abused by some in the church to extend their spiritual and temporal powers.

Newman was not against modernity *per se*; instead he favoured a neutral, tolerant and secular state which need not uphold the church.

71 Adrian Hastings, *The Theology of a Protestant Catholic* (Philadelphia: Trinity Press International, 1990), 117.
72 *Apologia pro Vita Sua*,
    http://www.newmanreader.org/works/apologia/correspondence.html, 6.
73 Owen Chadwick, *Newman* (Oxford: Oxford University Press, 1983), 60.

His view was far from conventional in that he believed a decline in religious beliefs would not affect the morality of the people. Far in advance of his time, Newman stressed the role of the laity in the church and the need for a Catholic intellectual renaissance. On the development of doctrine, Newman was considered a liberal in the Catholic Church when he acknowledged the historical and sociological factors and circumstances in the formation of dogmas.

In the next chapter I will begin with a short biography of Newman focussing on the early influence, especially at Oxford, which moulded his religious attitude, as well as the Oxford Movement in which he played a key role in dealing with the onslaught of liberalism prevalent at that time. This is important for us to understand his stand on liberalism and the issues related to it. Newman was what Oxford made him: a scholar and a gentleman with a certain cultural and religious outlook.

Chapter 2

Biographical Sketch

In the course of his long life, John Henry Newman had had many con-
versions, and he changed his mind at least five times: from an adoles-
cent fling with atheism, to evangelical and Calvinistic Anglicanism,
liberalism at Oxford, High Church Tractarianism and finally to Roman
Catholicism. Little wonder that he says, 'In a higher world it is otherwise, but here below to live is to change, and to be perfect is to have
changed often'.[1] However, it seems that his attitude towards liberalism
remained constant throughout his entire life. We will trace his early
upbringing and the influence of Oxford that shaped his understanding
of liberalism.

Early Life

Newman lived a long life spanning almost the entire nineteenth century. He was born on 21 February 1801, in the City of London, and
died at Edgbaston, Birmingham, on 11 August 1890. His father was
John Newman and his mother Jemima Fourdrinier of French Hugue-
not stock, which accounts for his religious training in the form of
modified Calvinism received from his mother. As a child he was
brought up to take delight in Bible reading although he formed no religious conviction until he was fifteen when he underwent a 'conver-

---

1   *An Essay on the Development of the Christian Doctrine*,
     http://www.newmanreader.org/works/. development/index.html, 41.

sion', and from the works of Calvinistic writers, he gained definite dogmatic ideas.

Newman matriculated at Trinity College, Oxford, on December 1816. Working too hard for his degree, he suffered a nervous breakdown, and obtained only third-class honours in 1821. Nonetheless his intellectual gifts did not go unrecognised. Oriel was by repute the foremost of the Oxford Colleges, and Newman was elected a Fellow there on 12 April 1822. An intellectual and reforming college, Oriel chose its Fellows with great care from those individuals who had great academic abilities as well as qualities of mind and character which examinations could not detect. In this aspect, Newman's election as Fellow was a noteworthy academic achievement.[2] He felt this to be the turning point of his life and the most memorable of all days. More crucially, it brought him in contact with the celebrated Noetics – intellectuals who insisted that reason and not authority was supreme. These were well-respected clergymen who became the pioneers of that liberal spirit in religion which Newman would later oppose. The Noetics were possibly the last English representatives of a school of Christian apologists who based their views on Locke's *An Essay Concerning Human Understanding*. They included Renn Dickson Hampden, Thomas Arnold, Baden Powell, Richard Whately and Joseph Blanco White. Their theological tools were dialectics, scripture and private judgment, and they adopted the anti-dogmatic principle. They disapproved of tradition, religious mystery, creeds and sacraments. The Noetics believed that traditional explanations of the Trinity and Incarnation were human speculation based on an outmoded form of scholasticism.[3]

Reason, for the Noetics, meant 'conscious, scientific, and methodical argument', and they undertook, not a 'critique of secular Reason in the name of faith', but a 'critique of faith in the name of Reason

2   Terrence Kenny, *The Political Thought of John Henry Newman* (London: Longman, Green and Co., 1957), 8.
3   Francis McGrath, *John Henry Newman: Universal Revelation* (Mulgrave, Victoria: John Garratt Publishing, 1977), 51.

and its claim to measure all realities, natural and divine alike'.[4] Their stated aim for doing this was supposed to defend Christianity against rationalism. But in doing so, faith was reduced to little more than a game of logical deduction. They and their followers would eventually reject any notion of the supernatural or mystery element in religion because reason could not deal with the unknown. Newman, who by nature and temperament, thrived in mysticism, would oppose this critique of faith in the name of reason.

The Noetics were confident of their intellectual prowess and set out to solve all problems solely by the light of reason. They delighted in criticising and questioning every religious and ecclesiastical issue. Naturally, they grew weary of church authority and orthodoxy, as they separated the notions of sin and virtue from their religious context and conscience, and viewed them according to reason – everything that was thought to be from God was now viewed in human terms.[5]

Nonetheless, the Noetics were loyal members of the Anglican Church with good intentions, and Walgrave argues that it was Newman's psychological genius that enabled him to foresee the conclusions of liberalism.[6] On the other hand, though, Newman's young, impressionable mind was also captivated by the rationalism of the Noetics. At the same time, with his mystical bend, he would finally conclude that the application of logic to faith as one of the greatest evils of the age.

Richard Whately, who later became Archbishop of Dublin, was a prominent Noetic who had an early influence on Newman. In the *Apologia pro Vita Sua*, Newman writes that the Oriel common room was a place that 'stank of logic'.[7] Kenny argues that it was not so much a reliance on formal logic as an overweening display of confidence in human reasoning and a contempt for tradition and authority which

---

4   Quoted in Terrence Merrigan, 'Newman's Oriel experience: its significance for his life and thought', *Bijdragen* 47, no. 2 (1986),193.

5   J.H. Walgrave, *Newman the Theologian* (London: Geoffrey Chapman, 1960), 33.

6   Ibid.

7   *Apologia pro Vita Sua*, http://www.newmanreader.org/works/apologia65/chapter4-1.html,169.

Newman found there.[8] Newman explicitly says it was Whately who taught him to think and to use his reason.[9] Thus, due to the influence of Whately, in those early years at Oriel, Newman's quest for intellectual excellence consumed his whole being, and forty years later he wrote: 'The truth is, I was beginning to prefer intellectual excellence to moral'.[10] It was this excessive reliance on intellect, to the neglect of moral consideration that led Newman to label it as 'liberalism'.

Besides Whately, Hawkins, another Fellow and later Provost of Oriel, helped to sharpen Newman's intellectual powers. Newman helped greatly in preparing Whately's *Elements of Logic* which Terrence Kenny thinks was used as an anvil for Whately to forge his ideas. Hawkins took great care to criticise any looseness of thought and expression in Newman. Thus, for the rest of his life Newman was always conscious to make sure that his words represented his idea clearly: he is 'the master of words, and not they of him'.[11] In spite of his later opposition to that certain liberal spirit in religion, the liberal influence of the Noetics did make a lasting impression on Newman.

Even before leaving his curacy at St Clement to accept his tutorship in Oriel, Newman was drifting away from Evangelicalism and towards an anti-dogmatic liberalism characterised as a 'cold Arminian doctrine' typical of the Noetics.[12] It is not an exaggeration to say Newman did dally with liberalism and labelled it 'Whatelyan'. In one of his sermons he suggests Christian liberty consists in our knowing 'the reasons of the divine commands' which means going against blind obedience, and that in the gospels, Christ gives us the principles

8   Terrence Kenny, *The Political Thought of John Henry Newman* (London: Longman, Green and Co., 1957), 8.
9   *Apologia pro Vita Sua,*
     http://www.newmanreader.org/works/apologia65/chapter1.html, 11.
10   Ibid.,14.
11   Terrence Kenny, *The Political Thought of John Henry Newman* (London: Longman, Green and Co.,1957), 9.
12   Francis McGrath, *John Henry Newman: Universal Revelation* (Mulgrave, Victoria: John Garratt Publishing, 1977), 18. Arminian Theology, named after James Arminius (1560-1609), emphasizes human freedom of choices, whereas traditional Calvinism emphasizes the absolute sovereignty of God.

which act as foundations for 'knowledge of our duty, as sanctions for enforcing it upon us, and as motives for our performing it'.[13] In another sermon, he says the Trinity 'is not one doctrine, but a set of doctrines, collected together and viewed in a particular light by the Church'; that 'it is scriptural facts reduced to order by man'; that 'our rational belief in it becomes a test of our having examined it carefully and humbly'; and that 'it seems intended to teach us that our belief in it must be practical, and not merely intellectual and abstract'.[14]

Break with Liberalism at Oxford

Newman eventually began to doubt the power of reason to understand divine mystery. Well aware of the danger of using reason to arrive at religious truth, he writes in *Parochial and Plain Sermons*, that there are pitfalls threatening intellectually-gifted people:

> But when that gift of reason is something especial – clear, brilliant, or powerful, – then our danger is increased. The first sin of men of superior understanding is to value themselves upon it, and look down upon others. They make intellect the measure of praise and blame... Having thus cast down moral excellence from its true station, and set up the usurping empire of mere reason, next, they place a value upon all truths exactly in proportion to the possibility of proving them by means of that mere reason.[15]

According to Terrence Merrigan, Newman's break with liberalism in 1830 was based on his university sermons preached before the University of Oxford. Here he insisted mere intellect cannot foster true spiritual life. This is because Newman was too deeply rooted in his belief in the objective truth of Christian revelation to be influenced by

13   Quoted in Francis McGrath, *John Henry Newman: Universal Revelation* (Mulgrave, Victoria : John Garratt Publishing, 1977), 39.
14   Ibid.
15   *Parochial and Plain Sermons*, http://www.newmanreader.org/ works/parochial /volume1/ sermon17.html, 1:223-224.

the religious ideal of liberalism.[16] My point, however, is that it was specifically religious liberalism Newman was trying to break off, not liberalism *per se*. Bearing in mind that Newman was young and impressionable where he was under the tutelage of Whately, he would have inherited some of that liberal spirit that remained with him throughout his life.

His opposition to religious liberalism also included a specific reaction to a particular individual. In November 1834, Hampden sent to Newman a pamphlet advocating the admission of religious dissenters into Oxford University. In this pamphlet, among other things, Hampden wrote that doctrines are merely 'conclusions of human reasoning' and are not strictly speaking 'religious truths'. So, why should we prevent those who hold different theological views from entering the university?[17] Newman thought Hampden's pamphlet would 'make a shipwreck of Christian faith' and disrupt peace and harmony at Oxford. Thirty years later, Newman recalled that Hampden's pamphlet was the first assault made by the Anglican liberalism on the 'old orthodoxy of Oxford and England'.[18] Ironically, this opening up of Oxford to people of all creeds and beliefs became a reality, and it was Newman's departure from the Anglican Church that disrupted peace and harmony at Oxford.

Newman's secession from the Anglican Church would not have occurred if he had not learned to think for himself. That he was able to change the church of his birth to embrace the Roman communion without legal or ecclesiastical hindrances was due in part to the growing liberal atmosphere in England in the 1840s and also to Newman's independent thinking which he inherited at Oriel. He was an intellectual who spoke about the danger of putting too much trust in the intellect and the use of reason in religious matters. But as we shall see, his

16   Terrence Merrigan, 'Newman's Oriel experience: its significance for his life and thought', *Bijdragen* 47, no. 2 (1986),195.
17   Francis McGrath, *John Henry Newman: Universal Revelation* (Mulgrave, Victoria: John Garratt Publishing, 1977), 52.
18   *Apologia pro Vita Sua*, http://www.newmanreader.org/works/apologia65/chapter2.html, 57-58.

writings reveal his clarity of thought and intellectual brilliance, as well as possessing a liberal temper, even among the theological works.

Newman's years of association with the Noetics provided him with insights and ideas on liberalism, some of which he rejected and others he accepted, consciously and unconsciously. He had a certain 'intuitive genius' in perceiving the essence and direction of any philosophical trend, and Merrigan argues that it is this intellectual acuity that allowed Newman to foresee secularism or the unbelief inherent in liberalism.[19] But this is speculative because one could be a liberal and hold strong religious convictions as well. As I have explained earlier, Newman opposed certain aspects of liberalism and not the entire concept behind the term, and this particular spirit of liberalism is the tendency towards scepticism that dominated university culture in the second half of the nineteenth century. He was aware of the danger and threat posed to the Christian faith, but he also believed it would not affect the general morals of the people.

The liberalism that Newman was exposed to at Oxford was also a form of rationalism based on the primacy of reason. This means that knowledge of things from outside is the supreme force of life and that impartial reason can govern our human conduct. Newman, on the other hand, insisted that conscience which speaks to us at the depths of our hearts is the sole instrument that can help us discern the truth in religion and judge those first principles. He also understood that conscience is an instrument of knowledge whose effectiveness depends on one's moral integrity and purity. This does not mean that Newman was opposed to reason or high culture which sustained a high standard of intellectual endeavours. In fact, as a member of the intellectual elite, his writings display a brilliant use of reason, and in his *The Idea of a University*, he sings the praises of high culture which promotes intellectual excellence.

What Newman strongly opposed was the superficial use of reason to areas it did not belong – the religious sphere. He was aware that

---

19 Terrence Merrigan, 'Newman's Oriel experience: its significance for his life and thought', *Bijdragen* 47, no. 2 (1986),196.

pride, 'the subtlest and most rooted vice of the human mind', assists this shallow application of rational thought to spiritual things, and history has shown that 'the temptation of rationalism becomes the gravest of all for sinful man'.[20] Newman always considered that reason when applied to religion acts as a solvent and promotes hostility towards religious faith. This is why he reached the conclusion that dogmatic religion requires an infallible authority. This realization of the shortcomings of liberalism was gradual: the result of a series of events that took place after his appointment as tutor of Oriel College in 1826. He would say later that his sickness in November 1827 'broke me off from an incipient liberalism' and he claimed to be unable to 'think or recollect' during that period; the sickness brought home to him the fragility of the intellect. He discovered that 'the intellect he had begun to rely on too much was only an instrument, and could in a moment go horribly wrong, leaving him helpless'.[21] It is likely that Newman came out of this illness with a profound sense of the relative value of the intellect and decided to be more devout. The liberalism that Newman claimed to have broken off is one that stressed the supremacy of the intellect and discounted the grace of God. We would not call it liberalism today, but pride or 'Pelagianism'.

As well as illness, bereavement led Newman away from his flirtation with liberalism. The death of his youngest sister, Mary, in January 1828, caused him to realise in a more profound manner the 'transitory nature of this world', and revived his 'sense of the overpowering reality' of the unseen world.[22] He writes, 'What a veil and curtain this world of sense is! Beautiful, but still a veil'.[23] In 1823, he concluded that material phenomena, while undeniably real, were 'sacramentally connected with [a] more momentous system' and in 1827, upon reading John Keble's *The Christian Year*, he then regarded material phe-

---

20   J.H. Walgrave, *Newman The Theologian* (London: Geoffrey Chapman, 1960), 35.
21   Quoted in Terrence Merrigan, 'Newman's Oriel experience: its significance for his life and thought', *Bijdragen* 47, no. 2 (1986),196.
22   Ibid.
23   Ibid., 197.

nomena as 'both the types and the instruments of real things unseen'.[24] His sister's death turned his mind to the spiritual world beyond the sense and intellect, and he understood the limits of rational discourse, as Merrigan argues.[25] But this in no way shows that he became an anti-liberal.

It is true that Newman had already adopted a 'dogmatic' faith, which accounts for his final renunciation of the kind of liberalism propagated by the Noetics and their successors in Oxford. He understood the plight of the world and mankind's miseries: human's condition is a 'heart-piercing, reason-bewildering fact', which 'seems simply to give the lie to that great truth' of God's existence.[26] He was aware of the inability of liberalism to give answers to the mysteries of life and death, and this was reinforced by his growing appreciation of the Catholic faith and contacts with Fellows other than the Noetics, and also by his discovery of the Patristic Fathers.

Newman's theological developments grew out of these encounters, and during his Oriel years he gained the conviction that proper moral dispositions were indispensable for growing in faith. This led him to assign reason to its proper place, but not to discount it altogether. He was not anti-intellectual and did not reject liberalism entirely; he merely sought to give reason an appropriate role regarding the understanding of the Christian religion.

The experience at Oriel was crucial in the development of Newman's personality. He was aware of the danger of rationalising religion, but at the same time he was fascinated by the liberal intellectual culture of Oxford, and was even seduced by it for a while. Here Newman witnessed the opposition between liberalism and religious ethos, but as a sensitive young man he was too deeply rooted in his faith and his fear of divine judgment to decide in favour of reason without taking conscience into consideration. Nonetheless, the liberal

24   Ibid.
25   Ibid. 196.
26   *Apologia pro Vita Sua*,
      http://www.newmanreader.org/works/apologia65/chapter5.html, 241.

spirit of Oxford in different shades remained with him and manifested itself in some of his ideas on educational and ecclesiastical matters.

John Keble and Hurrell Froude

Besides the Noetics, there were two people, John Keble and Hurrell Froude, who had made a deep impact on Newman and taught him a religious ideal which was in sharp contrast to the liberalism at Oxford. Keble, who influenced Newman profoundly, was a model of piety and sought to lessen Oriel's liberal drift. In the *Apologia*, Newman says, 'in and from Keble the mental activity of Oxford took that contrary direction which issued in what was called Tractarianism'.[27] He meant that Keble's thinking went in the opposite direction of liberalism for he was a man who had few sympathies with the liberal party known as 'intellectuals', and he provided Newman an ideal of Christian holiness:

> Keble was young in years, when he became a University celebrity, and younger in mind. He had the purity and simplicity of a child. He had few sympathies with the intellectual party, who sincerely welcomed him as a brilliant specimen of young Oxford. He instinctively shut up before literary display, and pomp and donnishness of manner, faults which always will beset academic notabilities.[28]

Keble believed that intellectual gifts were in danger of being over-prized at the expense of sound moral judgment which he defined as 'a sound perception of the chief good together with a real and steady wish to obtain it',[29] and thus he set ethos above intellect, a teaching

---

27 *Apologia pro Vita Sua,*
    http://www.newmanreader.org/works/apologia65/notea.html, 189.
28 Ibid., 289-290.
29 Quoted in Terrence Merrigan, 'Newman's Oriel experience: its significance for his life and thought', *Bijdragen* 47, no. 2 (1986),199.

contrary to the principle of the intellectual liberal party at Oxford. Kenny argues that the liberal influence in the Oriel Common Room was not inconsistent with the Tory influence of Keble who perhaps was wary of Newman's incipient liberalism.[30]

Newman was not against the liberalism of Oxford as such, but as an ardent admirer of Keble, he happened to share some of his anti-intellectual tendency. I believe Newman was attracted to Keble as an example of Christian holiness, and not so much to Keble's thought. In spite of their protest against overprizing intellectual excellence, both men were brilliant intellectuals, and even the 'intellectual party sincerely welcomed Keble as a brilliant specimen of young Oxford', as we have seen earlier. It was only in this liberal atmosphere at Oxford that Newman and Keble could flourish in their own ways, and in many ways they were products of this liberal spirit which they thought they were fighting against.

Froude possessed a much more logical and critical intellect than Keble, and was also keenly interested in the 'ethos' in religious traditions. Froude viewed history in moral terms, and thus, he regarded the English Reformers with suspicion, thought of them as men of questionable integrity, and judged the English Reformation negatively.[31] Froude believed that rebellion against the Catholic ethos and the spirit of reverence and awe, which characterised the Reformation, would eventually lead to the rationalism that was now threatening England. Under the influence of Keble, Froude deepened his High Church convictions and experienced a profound religious awakening. It was from Froude that Newman began to look towards the Church of Rome with its unique practices, such as devotion to the Blessed Virgin Mary.[32]

30   Terrence Kenny, *The Political Thought of John Henry Newman* (London: Longman, Green and Co., 1957), 10.
31   Terrence Merrigan, 'Newman's Oriel experience: its significance for his life and thought', *Bijdragen* 47, no. 2 (1986),199.
32   *Apologia pro Vita Sua*, http://www.newmanreader.org/works/apologia65/chapter1.html, 25.

According to Merrigan, Froude's greatest influence on Newman was his emphasis on the priority of the moral dimension in religious matters.[33] In March 1828, Newman wrote about subordinating the intellect to ethos, claiming to have been influenced by Froude:

> Intellect seems to me but the attendant and servant of right moral feeling in this [sic] own weak and dark state of being - defending it when attacked, accounting for it, and explaining it in a poor way to others.[34]

The point Newman was making is that mere external evidence provided by logical demonstration was not enough to convince people about the truth of Christianity. What we need is a kind of 'internal evidence', a disposition to believe in favour of faith, and this can come about through moral feeling. In one of his university sermons at Oxford, Newman speaks about moral feeling as those 'previous notices prepossessions, and (in a good sense of the word) prejudice'[35] that lead the individual to admit the 'antecedent probability' of the Christian religion.[36] Following one's conscience and the practice of moral life determined our nature as Newman says it so simply – 'a good and a bad man will think very different things probable'.[37]

The Church Fathers

Besides the men living with him, there were also those from the past that influenced Newman deeply in his religious and theological think-

33   Terrence Merrigan, 'Newman's Oriel experience: its significance for his life and thought', *Bijdragen* 47, no. 2 (1986),200.
34   Quoted in Terrence Merrigan, 'Newman's Oriel experience its significance for his life and thought', *Bijdragen* 47, no. 2 (1986),200.
35   *Oxford University Sermons*,
    http://www.newmanreader.org/works/oxford/sermon10.html, 187.
36   Ibid., 195.
37   Ibid., 191.

ing. These were the Fathers of the early church, particularly Clement of Alexandria and Origen: two leading exponents of the movement to 'reconcile divine Truth with human Reason' by promoting secular learning and pursuing it within the framework of moral and religious training.[38] These early Church Fathers were convinced that mere learning was insufficient to provide impetus for moral action, and thus, the Alexandria school became a place for training in virtues. In the *Apologia*, Newman records that the Alexandrian Fathers exercised a special attraction for him, and he treats of their significance for his thinking:

> The broad philosophy of Clement and Origen carried me away; the philosophy, not the theological doctrine; and I have drawn out some features of it in my volume, with the zeal and freshness, but with the partiality, of a neophyte.[39]

Clement was a Christian Platonist and humanist who tried to reconcile Christianity and Hellenism. He believed they shared a common tradition.[40] Through reading the Church Fathers, Newman began to accept that everyone including pagans, had a personal conscience from which they could derive 'the knowledge of a Creator and Governor of the world, and of the general duty of virtue'.[41] If we follow these principles faithfully, there is 'no limit to the power of natural conscience'[42] in teaching us about our moral duty independent of Christian revelation.

In some ways the Church Fathers can be regarded as liberals in the sense that they were not fundamentalists and there was a degree of openness in the way they viewed scripture and the world. To the

---

38 Quoted in Terrence Merrigan, 'Newman's Oriel experience: its significance for his life and thought', *Bijdragen* 47, no. 2 (1986), 201.

39 *Apologia pro Vita Sua*,
http://www.newmanreader.org/works/apologia65/chapter1.html, 26.

40 Francis McGrath, *John Henry Newman: Universal Revelation* (Victoria: John Garratt Publishing, 1977), 46.

41 Quoted in Francis McGrath, *John Henry Newman: Universal Revelation* (Victoria: John Garratt Publishing, 1977), 41.

42 Ibid.

Church Fathers, 'Nature was a parable: Scripture was an allegory: pagan literature, philosophy, and mythology, properly understood, were but a preparation for the Gospel'.[43] The influence of the Church Fathers on Newman's theology of religions will be discussed later.

It should be stressed that the Church Fathers' insistence on virtue did not mean that they rejected intellectual pursuit – there is no sign of anti-intellectualism in their writings. Christianity to them was the perfection of the secular world, and the Fathers set forth 'as an ideal the development of man's rational powers – his reason, imagination and taste', which Newman would later call the 'philosophic habit of mind'. In the context of the moral life, intellectual excellence was a desirable goal to pursue, for the Fathers were interested in the development of the whole person – mind, heart and will.[44]

Newman was definitely influenced by this teaching of the Fathers: the development of the whole person. This, I believe, is the liberal spirit in the truest sense which Newman imbued, and he stood firmly in this tradition by confronting rationalistic and utilitarian principles hostile to religion by insisting that academic and scientific studies must be complemented by moral and religious education.

The religious philosophy of Clement and Origen also influenced profoundly Newman's own metaphysical intuition which Walgrave regards as Platonic because it holds the visible world as a veil hiding from us the invisible world.[45] Newman was led to believe that our knowledge of the world was at best a shadowy representation of the realities which are incomprehensible to human beings. Ideas are infinite, but our language is limited in trying to express them. At the same time our mind could grasp more than it could express, and it could also grasp more than it was conscious of holding.[46] This is also a

43   *Apologia pro Vita Sua,*
     http://www.newmanreader.org/works/apologia65/chapter1.html, 27.
44   Terrence Merrigan, 'Newman's Oriel experience: its significance for his life and thought', *Bijdragen* 47, no. 2 (1986), 202.
45   J.H. Walgrave, *Newman the Theologian* (London: Geoffrey Chapman, 1960), 18.
46   Terrence Kenny, *The Political Thought of John Henry Newman* (London: Longman, Green and Co., 1957), 49.

Christian conception, and Newman felt he was able to discern the spiritual universe at the heart of the concrete reality of the world – 'a mystical presence shining through the visible form and perceived by a sensibility at once poetical and religious'.[47] This Platonism affected him deeply and inspired many of his university sermons. He thought the Platonic idea of pre-existence was a 'most beautiful doctrine' and one that could be modified to suit Christian theology.[48]

At the same time, Newman was also influenced by a typically English feature, the taste for the concrete and real – empiricism. Hence we find in Newman a Platonic longing counterpoised by his English temperament of love for facts, perceived and verified. Walgrave added that his study of Aristotle helped in preventing Newman from reaching certain extreme conclusions drawn from a Platonic standpoint.[49] Nonetheless, Newman's Platonism is important for us to understand his theory of development, the concept of growth and analogy.

The Oxford Movement

It is not surprising that Newman's intellectual formation took place during his initial period at Oxford, and in the *Apologia*, he describes in detail the influence of Hawkins and Whately in the Oriel Common Room. Under Whately, he came to accept the idea that the church was an independent organization, which is of great importance for his later works. It is this anti-erastianism, a view that opposes the subordination of the church to the state that led to the founding of the Oxford Movement.[50] Through the influence of Keble and of Butler's *Analogy*

---

47   J.H. Walgrave, *Newman the Theologian* (London: Geoffrey Chapman, 1960), 18.
48   Francis McGrath, *John Henry Newman: Universal Revelation* (Mulgrave, Victoria: John Garratt Publishing, 1977), 92.
49   J.H. Walgrave, *Newman the Theologian* (London: Geoffrey Chapman, 1960), 18.
50   Ibid., 31.

of Religion, Newman discovered the fundamental Christian sacramental principle. At the same time, he was also drawn to ponder over the problem of the basis of belief and religious certitude, which eventually became his life-long concern.

In 1826, Newman was appointed a tutor at Oriel, but was forced to resign in 1832 due to a conflict with Hawkins, the Provost. That same year, he made a journey to the Mediterranean, visiting Malta, Italy, Corfù and Sicily together with Hurrell Froude and Froude's father. He fell seriously ill when he returned to Sicily by himself, and when he returned to England, he was convinced that God kept him alive because he had a mission to fulfil:

> 'We have a work to do in England'. I went down at once to Sicily, and the presentiment grew stronger. I struck into the middle of the island, and fell ill of a fever at Leonforte. My servant thought that I was dying, and begged for my last directions. I gave them, as he wished; but I said, 'I shall not die'. I repeated, 'I shall not die, for I have not sinned against light, I have not sinned against light'. I never have been able quite to make out what I meant.[51]

Newman returned from Italy believing he had a mission to fight the so-called liberalism of Oxford. The Church of England had become an organ of the state, its life depended on secular powers in which the members of the government might not be Anglicans or Christians for that matter, and yet they had the power to control the church. During this time, the state exercised control over the church for political reasons; for example in 1833, Parliament suppressed ten Irish bishoprics because it thought them superfluous. Thus, it was urgent for the church to be independent from state control. Newman, encouraged by Froude, proposed to restore the church back to its pristine condition, separated from the state, and based on apostolic succession. In Newman's view, the battle against political liberalism was secondary; the main purpose of the movement was to combat liberalism in philoso-

---

51   *Apologia pro Vita Sua*,
      http://www.newmanreader.org/works/apologia65/chapter1.html, 34-35.

phy and religion which he believed was undermining the Christian faith.[52]

In his relatively uneventful life as Fellow of Oriel, Newman had time to read the Church Fathers and early church history which led him to appreciate authority and to value dogma. Newman sought to have her God-given authority restored to the Church of England. He was convinced that this church must be dogmatic because she had truths that needed to be protected. The church must not only safeguard and teach the truth, but also single out and condemn error. For Newman, the Oxford Movement was a religious enterprise attempting to uphold the objective religious truth, dogma, against the onslaught of subjectivism and relativism.[53]

As the animating and driving force of the Oxford Movement, Newman played an influential role in the effort to return the Anglican Church to the foundations of the faith through emphasis on the sacraments, episcopal governance, and apostolic succession, in order to combat the liberal tendency of spiritual liberty and private judgment. The Movement began on July 14, 1833, when John Keble delivered a sermon entitled 'National Apostasy' from the pulpit of St. Mary's, Oxford. The members of this movement were also known as 'Tractarians'. Newman contributed twenty-four tracts in the series known as the *Tracts of the Times*, expressing his desire to see a revival in the Church of England based on Catholic principles.

It is important to note that the Movement began as a counterattack against the advance of liberalism, but logically ended as a revolutionary attack on Protestantism based on its Catholic principles. Liberalism began to spread deeper and deeper into the intellectual, cultural, political and religious life in England. Late Victorian England was liberal – rights were guaranteed regardless of beliefs, universities became independent of the Established Church, there was general acceptance that reason and social utility should prevail over tradition and

---

52   J.H. Walgrave, *Newman The Theologian* (London: Geoffrey Chapman, 1960), 36.
53   Terrence Kenny, *The Political Thought of John Henry Newman* (London: Longman, Green and Co.,1957), 49.

authority. Freedom of conscience and expression was present.[54] These were positive aspects of liberalism which nobody could deny, and it was in this liberal society that Catholics in England would eventually have their rights and freedom to worship. When Newman was born, it was not a liberal society, but it gradually became one. Newman was fortunate to experience this freedom of the time because it was in this liberal atmosphere that the *Catholic Relief Act* (1829) and the Restoration of the Catholic Hierarchy in England took place in 1850.

The Oxford Movement tried to stop the onslaught of liberalism by reviving Catholic piety and restoring the ancient faith and practice. The leaders of this movement were not innovators and they distrusted novelty; liberal change was regarded as apostasy by the Tractarians. James C. Livingston argues that the movement was not a mere repetition of the teachings of the Church Fathers, but a 'creative restatement of the ancient verities' as exemplified by Newman, and he regards the Tractarians as Romantics who had a strong feeling for the beauty of nature, the mystery of medievalism, respect for authority and tradition.[55] The Tractarians also placed emphasis on the sacramental principle, and the Incarnation, the sanctifying of our fallen human nature, is spoken in relation to the 'ministration of the Sacraments'.[56] This sacramental principle encouraged the use of sacramental forms and inculcated a greater reverence for the church as a divine instrument for imparting God's grace.[57]

The Tractarians possessed a deep sense of the holy mysteries of God in contrast to the scientific and logical outlook of the liberals at Oxford. Newman in particular had a strong mystical feeling for the actuality of the supernatural and the invisible world of angels and spirits as he expresses it in his sermons on 'The Invisible World':

54 See Adrian Hastings, *The Theology of a Protestant Catholic* (Philadelphia: Trinity Press International, 1990), 116.
55 James C. Livingston, *Modern Christian Thought* (New Jersey: Prentice Hall, 1997), 168.
56 Ibid., 179.
57 Ibid., 181.

Even when it is gayest, with all its blossoms on, and shows most touchingly what lies hid in it, yet it is not enough. We know much more lies hid in it than we see. A world of Saints and Angels, a glorious world, the palace of God, the mountain of the Lord of Hosts, the heavenly Jerusalem, the throne of God and Christ, all these wonders, everlasting, all-precious, mysterious, and incomprehensible, lie hid in what we see ... We know that what we see is as a screen hiding from us God and Christ, and His Saints and Angels. And we earnestly desire and pray for the dissolution of all that we see, from our longing after that which we do not see....[58]

In the sermons, 'Mysteries in Religion', 'The Indwelling Spirit', 'The Gospel, a Trust Committed to Us', 'Tolerance of Religious Error', and 'Christian Zeal', Newman believes that mystery affects every moment of our lives.[59] The growing trend among the liberals at that time was that creeds and articles of faith were just opinions. They damaged genuine religion, and belief in them was superstitious. But Newman thought otherwise. He insisted that we should receive articles of creed with awe and reverence because they are mysterious and beyond human understanding. We do not have to understand them in order to believe them – it is the work of the Holy Spirit and we must silently worship and faithfully preserve them. Newman also believed faith is a deposit of theological propositions that remains the same in every age, and every article of the creed is derived from scripture.[60]

Tractarians believed that our sense experience and ideas are pale expressions of the spiritual truths that we try to approximate. Christians need to let go of these sensory perceptions in order to understand the transitory nature of this world. The world is a veil hiding the mysteries of the supernatural realm, and Christians should not be afraid to believe in a way that may seem credulous in the eyes of the world. Newman asserts that if one considers nature as baffling, then it is un-

58   *Parochial and Plain Sermons*,
      http://www.newmanreader.org/works/parochial/volume4/sermon13.html,
      IV: 210-211.
59   Ibid., II: 206-16; 217-31; 255-73; 274-90; 379-92.
60   Francis McGrath, *John Henry Newman: Universal Revelation* (Mulgrave, Victoria: John Garratt Publishing, 1977), 53.

derstandable that the Trinity and the Incarnation, being the highest mysteries of faith, are not rationally explicable and must be approached with reverent awe.[61]

The seat of authority is to be found in the ancient traditions and official teachings of the church, the Tractarians taught. The Oxford leaders looked to tradition as a bulwark against the inundation of liberal individualism. Appeal could no longer be made to 'Scripture alone' – 'the Bible was the cause, not the cure of sectarian division'.[62] Eventually this would lead to criticising the Protestant Reformers whose battle cry against the Catholic Church was '*Sola Scriptura*'. There was a need to have a strong base to combat the secular state and erastianism in the church, and the returning to the ancient church with its apostolic succession appealed to the Tractarians. The theme of apostolic succession was a common theme in the early tracts and it was the first principle of the movement. Newman writes:

> The royal dynasty of the Apostles is far older than all the kingly families which are now on the earth. Every Bishop of the Church whom we behold, is a lineal descendant of St. Peter and St. Paul after the order of a spiritual birth ... He [Christ] has continued the line of His Apostles onwards through every age and all troubles and perils of the world. Here then, surely, is somewhat of encouragement for us amid our loneliness and weakness. The presence of every Bishop suggests a long history of conflicts and trials, sufferings and victories, hopes and fears, through many centuries. His presence at this day is the fruit of them all. He is the living monument of those who are dead. He is the promise of a bold fight and a good confession and a cheerful martyrdom now, if needful, as was instanced by those of old time. We see their figures on our walls, and their tombs are under our feet; and we trust, nay, we are sure, that God will be to us in our day what He was to them.[63]

---

61 See *Parochial and Plain Sermons*,
    http://www.newmanreader.org/works/parochial/volume1/index.html.
62 James C. Livingston, *Modern Christian Thought* (New Jersey: Prentice Hall, 1997), 171.
63 *Parochial and Plain Sermons*,
    http://www.newmanreader.org/works/parochial/volume3/.sermon17.html, III: 247-248.

Apostolic succession and the tradition found in the teachings of the Church Fathers, thus, constitute the argument in favour of church authority. The most important statement is found in Newman's *Lectures on the Prophetical Office of the Church, Viewed Relatively to Romanism and Popular Protestantism* (1837). Here he states that Protestantism's *Sola Scriptura* and the Catholic teaching of infallibility are historically untenable. He believed that unaided human reason is not capable of interpreting the Bible properly, and private judgment concerning scripture is no ground of authority – it leads only to chaos and division.

The Tractarians believed that the Scriptures were originally not systematic essays on Christian doctrines, but were received by Christian communities as the unwritten faith of the church. Newman was concerned about the means which direct our choice of interpreting the Scriptures. Besides experience and reason, he argued that the church and tradition also have a crucial role. All the Tractarians taught that the ancient tradition was needed to guide us in interpreting the Scriptures – the church guides us in the proper understanding of the Bible. In fact, before the establishment of the canons of the New Testament, the unwritten tradition guided the apostles' own writings. The Tractarians agreed with Roman Catholic teaching that authority rested in the Scriptures and the ancient traditions of the church. In *The Prophetical Office*, Newman sums up the view of the Tractarians:

> Let us understand what is meant by saying that Antiquity is of authority in religious questions. Both the Roman school and ourselves maintain as follows: That whatever doctrine the primitive ages unanimously attest, whether by consent of Fathers, or by Councils, or by the events of history, or by controversies, or in whatever way, whatever may fairly and reasonably be considered to be the universal belief of those ages, is to be received as coming from the Apostles ... The Rule or Canon which I have been explaining, is best known as expressed in the words of Vincentius of Lerins, in his celebrated treatise upon the tests of Heresy and Error; viz. that that is to be received as Apostolic which has been taught

'always, everywhere, and by all'. Catholicity, Antiquity, and consent of Fathers, is the proper evidence of the fidelity or Apostolicity of a professed Tradition.[64]

Livingston remarks that in an age where modern historical-critical research was popular, the Tractarians could still assert the canon of antiquity as the foundation of the authority of the church. They accepted the unity of the apostolic tradition because they were convinced that there was an original revelation given to us as means of our salvation. They were certain of the historicity of the unwritten tradition of the apostolic church and believed that the historical facts could be established using scientific tools of research; hence, there could be no good reason for radical skepticism which the liberals taught.[65]

Road to Rome

Except for Newman, the Tractarians' view of history was primitive and static. The theory of evolution and organic growth was being propagated in Europe at this time. It was 'the period of Hegelian ascendancy on the Continent, but the Oxford leaders did not read the Hegelian theologians, not even the Catholic Johann Adam Möhler', Livingston claims.[66] Newman, however, was different, and this reveals his genius and originality, and perhaps his liberal temper. In the summer of 1839 while working on the history of the Monophysite controversy, he was forced to rethink his concept of the church and also his view of history. The result of this was his essay on *The Development of Christian Doctrine*, a work wherein Newman rejects the

---

64   *The Prophetical Office*,
      http://www.newmanreader.org/works/viamedia/volume1/lecture2.html, 50-51.
65   James C. Livingston, *Modern Christian Thought* (New Jersey: Prentice Hall, 1997), 173.
66   Ibid., 174.

static Tractarian concept of history and supports an organic evolutionary theory of doctrinal development.

This work paved his way into the Roman Catholic Church although it was considered dangerous and liberal by some conservative Catholics. It does seem ironic that a liberal understanding of history as evolutionary and organic led Newman into the Roman Catholic Church which was perceived by his contemporaries as backward, superstitious, and a bastion of conservative and reactive forces trying to ward off the impact of modernism and secularism by closing upon itself.

So it was in 1839 that Newman began to lose confidence in the cause of the Oxford Movement which he had given so much of his time and effort. His study of the Monophysites also raised questions about the validity of the *Via Media*, the attempt to find a middle ground between the excesses of Roman Catholicism and Protestantism. It was also in 1839 that Newman read an article by Wiseman on the Donatist heresy in the *Dublin Review*, and was shocked by the implications of this phrase from St Augustine: *securus judicat orbis terrarium,* which means the universal church is in its judgments secure of truth. He realised that the Church of England seemed to be outside the universal circle of faith – it lacked apostolic roots.[67] In reality, the Anglican Church is no less schismatic in its relationship to the historic Catholic faith than the Donatists and the Monophysites of the late third and early fourth centuries. Newman came to realise that, in spite of its own historic excesses and corruptions, the Roman Catholic Church remains closest in terms of spirit, doctrine, teachings, and traditions to the apostolic church and the church of the early Fathers.

Newman wrote the *Essay on Development of Christian Doctrine* prior to his conversion in 1845 for he wanted to explain that nineteenth century Roman Catholicism was the closest to the church of Athanasius in the fourth Century, and not a corrupt version of it.[68] He

67   Edward Norman, *Roman Catholicism in England* (Oxford: Oxford University Press, 1985), 98.
68   *An Essay on the Development of Christian Doctrine,*
      http://www.newmanreader.org/works/development/chapter2.html, 97-98.

wrote this book not to prove the authenticity of Roman Catholicism, but to answer a difficulty concerning its incompatibility with the early church.[69] He soon became convinced that Rome and not Canterbury was the home of the church of the apostles. Newman expressed his new findings in Tract Ninety, in which he argued that the Thirty-Nine Articles, the doctrinal statement of the Church of England, could be interpreted in a way that supported Roman Catholic doctrine. The Tract, published on February 27, 1841, was naturally opposed by the authorities of the Anglican Church, and was censured on March 15. It was a big blow for the movement and eventually led to Newman's rapid withdrawal from Oxford. Between July 1841 and September 1843, he moved from Oxford to a semi-monastic community at Littlemore, retracted the anti-Catholic statements he had published, and resigned his position at St. Mary's.

Newman as a Catholic: 1845 - 1890

On October 9, 1845, two years after leaving St Mary's, Newman was officially received into the Catholic Church, and ordained to the priesthood the following year. His contemporaries regarded Newman's conversion in 1845 as 'a decisive marker in Catholic resurgence'.[70] His contribution as a Catholic priest included the establishment of the Oratory of St. Philip Neri near Birmingham in 1848 and the creation of the Catholic University of Ireland, in which he served as rector from 1854 to 1858. Some of his major publications as a Catholic were *The Idea of University* (1852), a collection of the inaugural lectures for the Catholic University and other academic essays, *Apologia pro Vita Sua* (1864), his spiritual autobiography, *Parochial*

---

69   Ibid., 30.
70   Edward Norman, *Roman Catholicism in England* (Oxford: Oxford University Press, 1985), 97.

and Plain Sermons (1868), a new edition of his Anglican discourses, and *An Essay in Aid of a Grammar of Assent* (1870), a work on the philosophy of religion.

In 1859, Newman became editor of the *Rambler*, a Catholic Review founded in 1848, in which the educated liberal Catholic laity, among them the Cambridge historian, Lord Acton, could air their views without restraint on the issues of the day including those regarding religion and the church. The church authorities were unhappy with the tone of these articles, and Newman was compelled to resign after the appearance of two numbers. His forays into this area seriously compromised him, and his resignation did not lessen the hostility and suspicion of some in the church. Without his knowledge, extracts from his celebrated *On Consulting the Faithful in Matters of Doctrine* were translated into Latin and sent to Rome. They aroused suspicion and misunderstanding in the Vatican which lasted until 1867 because Wiseman failed to communicate to Rome the explanation given by Newman.[71]

The publication of *Apologia pro Vita Sua* in 1864 won for Newman the lasting regard of the English people, and he assumed the position of a moderate and conciliatory theologian in countering Ultramontanism. He thus contributed more than anyone else to the intellectual prestige of Catholics and to gaining the sympathy of the English public.[72] He led the intellectual rebirth of Catholicism and the struggle against not only the liberalism of his day, but also Ultramontanism, which advocated an extreme view of the role of church authority and *magisterium* pronouncements.

Newman's conversion was not a disruption or discontinuity of his ideas, but was due to circumstances and allegiance, for his view of the church remained consistent. Before his conversion, he regarded the Anglican Church as upholding the principles of the primitive church of the apostles. After his conversion, he regarded the church of the Fathers as embodied in the Church of Rome and not in the Church

71   J.H. Walgrave, *Newman The Theologian* (London: Geoffrey Chapman, 1960), 40.
72   Ibid., 41.

of England, which he believed was a modern version of an ancient heresy which he had studied and written about in 1832 in *Arians of the Fourth Century*. The idea of a national church in an apostatising state was repugnant to Newman because it was contrary to the universal authority of antiquity. He was converted to Catholicism because he believed it was the embodiment of the primitive church handed down by the apostles. It is important to note that he developed his ideas on his own and was not influenced by any school of thought. Intellectually isolated all his life, Newman was original in his ideas and writings, and this accounts for his religious genius.[73]

The Tractarians tried to find a new ecclesiology to replace the 'soft erastianism' which was undermining Christian society – they wanted the national church to protest against the liberal tide. Hastings says Newman left the Church of England for the Roman Catholic Church which was more 'consistently illiberal'.[74] This is disputable because Roman Catholicism is also evolving, albeit in a slower manner, and there is such a thing as liberal Catholicism with which Newman had certain affinity.

By the 1870s, Newman was recognised for his contributions by both the Anglican and Roman Catholic Churches. He was the first person to be elected to an honorary fellowship of Trinity College in 1877, and two years later, Pope Leo XII made him cardinal. In Rome, when Newman received his cardinal's hat in 1879, he summarised his lifelong resistance to liberalism: 'the doctrine that there is no positive truth in religion, but that one creed is as good as another'.[75] This aspect of liberalism is but one dimension of a philosophy that is complex and ever changing. In the second half of the century Newman had

---

73   Edward Norman, *Roman Catholicism in England* (Oxford: Oxford University Press, 1985), 98.

74   Adrian Hastings, *The Theology of a Protestant Catholic* (Philadelphia: Trinity Press International, 1990), 117.

75   *Biglietto speech*,
      http://www.newmanreader.org/works/addresses/file2.html#biglietto, 64.

more in common with liberal Catholicism than was generally admitted.[76]

In the next chapter we will examine directly what Newman has to say about liberalism, its attitudes and basic assumptions. It is these messages, taken out of context, that led many people to label Newman as anti-liberal.

76   Edward Norman, *Roman Catholicism in England* (Oxford: Oxford University Press, 1985), 99.

Chapter 3

A Critic of Liberalism

Newman was fighting against the spirit of liberalism in religion which was threatening his beloved church. It was a liberalism that promoted relativism in faith and morals, and denied positive truths and dogmatic principles by adopting a subjective and rationalistic approach to religion. On the occasion of his becoming a cardinal, Newman spoke of his lifelong battle with this liberalism:

> And, I rejoice to say, to one great mischief I have from the first opposed myself. For thirty, forty, fifty years I have resisted to the best of my powers the spirit of liberalism in religion. Never did Holy Church need champions against it more sorely than now, when, alas! it is an error overspreading, as a snare, the whole earth and on this great occasion, when it is natural for one who is in my place to look out upon the world, and upon Holy Church as in it, and upon her future, it will not, I hope, be considered out of place if I renew the protest against it when I have made so often.

> Liberalism in religion is the doctrine that there is no positive truth in religion, but that one creed is as good as another, and this is the teaching which is gaining substance and force daily. It is inconsistent with any recognition of any religion, as true. It teaches that all are to be tolerated, for all are matters of opinion. Revealed religion is not a truth, but a sentiment and a taste; not an objective fact, not miraculous; and it is the right of each individual to make it say just what strikes his fancy.[1]

Looking back at his long life, Newman singled out his opposition to the spirit of liberalism in religion as his life struggle. He had changed his mind on many religious issues, but this battle against religious lib-

---

1   *Biglietto* Speech,
     http://www.newmanreader.org/works/addresses/file2.html#biglietto, 64.

eralism remained constant throughout. The fight was actually a warning against the secularization of public life which Newman saw was
coming and it is here today.

Origin of Liberalism: The Arian Connection

Newman's first book, *Arians of the Fourth Century*, published in
1833, deals with history and heresy. He attempts to find a link between an ancient heresy and the liberalism of his time. Rowan Williams considers this work a 'brilliant argument, linking all sorts of
diverse phenomena ... built up on a foundation of complacent bigotry
and historical fantasy'.[2] Nonetheless, this work can help us to identify
the source of liberalism which Newman was opposing; the work can
be seen as reflecting the religious condition of nineteenth century England. Newman studied the heresy that contaminated Christian doctrine
in the fourth century and came to believe that history repeated itself in
the religious crisis of nineteenth century England. Robert Pattison argues that the passages of the Reform Bill and Hampden's lectures
(Brampton lectures delivered at Oxford, 1832) made Newman realised
that liberalism was an older error originated from Arianism – the anti-
dogmatic principle and development which he mentioned in his *Apologia*. In Newman's opinion, Arius is the father of liberalism, the first
one who denied the dogmatic principle; hence, the origins of Western
liberalism were located in early Christian dogmatics.[3] The Arians provided Newman with a model to show the importance of belief in society. It convinced him that belief dominates all our actions and influences history, and that to understand belief is to understand life itself.[4]
In the *Apologia*, Newman writes, 'I saw clearly, that in the history of

2   Rowan Williams, *Arius* (London: SCM Press, 2001), 5.
3   Robert Pattison, *The Great Dissent* (Oxford: Oxford University Press, 1991), 101.
4   Ibid., 102.

Arianism, the pure Arians were the Protestants, the semi-Arians were the Anglicans, and that Rome now was what it was then. The truth lay, not with the *Via Media*, but with what was called "the extreme party"'.[5]

The Arians' contest of first principle dealing with the most fundamental issues of belief attracted Newman. For him it was not only a question of correct dogma, but whether we need dogma or not. Arius denied the validity of dogma and his teaching had corrupted the fourth century. According to Pattison, 'Newman laboured over the corpse of Arianism so he might learn to treat the virulent error of anti-dogmatism, now reincarnated in liberal thought'.[6] Arius believed God is 'inexpressible' – this is the key word of his teaching and according to him nothing created can speak meaningfully about the Creator. For Arius, even Christ, created and subordinated to the Father, cannot grasp adequately the idea of God. Newman considered the Arians 'a party who had no fixed tenet',[7] and that Arius held the anti-dogmatic principle which eventually became the main feature of Western liberalism.

Arianism was also a philosophy like liberalism, and for Newman, philosophy cut off from dogma is superficial and dangerous. He asserts that the Arians promoted Platonism using Aristotelian logic: 'their Christ is only the demiurge of Plato and they studied the world he had made by the methods of Aristotle'.[8] Thus, the Arians taught classical philosophy disguised as Christian theology – their heresy is 'founded in a syllogism'.[9] In the fourth century, Athanasius defended the church against Arius by upholding the dogmatic principle, and Newman did the same in the nineteenth century: 'the Church should

---

5   *Apologia pro Vita Sua*,
    http://www.newmanreader.org/works/apologia65/chapter3.html, 139.
6   Robert Pattison, *The Great Dissent* (Oxford: Oxford University Press, 1991), 108.
7   *Arians of the Fourth Century*,
    http://www.newmanreader.org/works/arians/chapter2-5.html, 231.
8   Robert Pattison, *The Great Dissent* (Oxford: Oxford University Press, 1991), 113.
9   *Arians of the Fourth Century*,
    http://www.newmanreader.org/works/arians/chapter1-2.html, 28.

teach the truth, and then should appeal to Scripture in vindication of its own teaching'.[10] This means that only the church speaking dogmatically can preserve the true doctrine from contamination by heretics. The error of liberalism is that it had rejected the dogmatic principle and thus, had denied the truth. For Newman, the mind is made for truth, and correct belief and right action lead us to the truth.

The protagonists of the Oxford Movement saw their mission as rescuing the Church of England from the heresy of liberalism. In the early nineteenth century, the Anglican Church with an outdated system of government was faced with the problem of responding to the demands of modernity. It was in the political and religious upheavals of his time that Newman asked the vital question in his *Apologia* : 'how were we going to keep the church from being liberalised?' He writes,

> While I was engaged in writing my work upon the Arians, great events were happening at home and abroad, which brought out into form and passionate expression the various beliefs which had so gradually been winning their way into my mind. Shortly before, there had been a Revolution in France; the Bourbons had been dismissed: and I held that it was unchristian for nations to cast off their governors … Again, the great Reform Agitation was going on around me as I wrote … The vital question was, how were we to keep the Church from being liberalised?[11]

Newman did not think evangelicals were capable of saving the church from the liberals because they themselves had been moving away from the orthodox faith with their concern for individual conversion. In *Arians of the Fourth Century*, Newman was convinced the Church of England was engaged in the same struggle in maintaining orthodoxy and fighting against liberalism, and the Oxford Movement would help to restore her to its pristine state.

---

10   Ibid.,
         http://www.newmanreader.org/works/arians/chapter1-3.html, 50.
11   *Apologia pro Vita Sua*
         http://www.newmanreader.org/works/apologia65/chapter1.html, 30.

Arianism was influenced by sources of authority similar to liberalism of his time. Newman identifies Antioch as the birthplace of this heresy which was produced by a combination of judaising tendencies with the influence of Greek philosophy and sophist syllogistic mode of reasoning. The twin influences of Judaism and sophistry led the Antiochene church to hold the authority of its predecessors contemptuously; these influences on the Antiochene Church 'ended in teaching them to regard the ecclesiastical authorities of former times as on a level with the uneducated and unenlightened of their own days'.[12] This means the Antiochenes saw themselves as superior to the established ecclesiastical authority. This was the kind of attitude Newman saw as disregarding traditional authority of scripture and creed, and supporting the relativism and rationalism of the eighteenth and nineteenth centuries. The Antiochene Church substituted rational philosophy for Christian authority – this was the same charge Newman made against the liberals of his days.

While the Church of Antioch was influenced by the sophists and the Judaisers, the Alexandrian Church was the 'eclectic' school of philosophy, a mixture of the Middle and Neo-platonic philosophies prevailing at the time. Eclecticism implies a combination of Greek philosophy and other schools, and it was a 'a heresy which, even more than others, has shown itself desirous and able to conceal itself under the garb of sound religion, and to keep the form, while it destroys the spirit, of Christianity'.[13] Its features include:

> the denial of the exclusive divine mission and peculiar inspiration of the Scripture Prophets; accompanied the while with a profession of general respect for them as benefactors of mankind ... In its most specious form, it holds whatever is good and true in the various religions in the world, to have actually come from God.[14]

12 *Arians of the Fourth Century,*
http://www.newmanreader.org/works/arians/chapter1-2.html, 36.
13 Ibid.,
http://www.newmanreader.org/works/arians/chapter1-4.html, 103.
14 Ibid., 104.

This kind of rationalism and syncretism was common in some Christian denominations and Judaism as well. It was for Newman a characteristic of the religious spirit of the age and a 'cultural relativism inherent in eclecticism'.[15] Newman writes, 'Who does not recognise in this old philosophy the chief features of that recent school of liberalism and false illumination, political and moral, which is now Satan's instrument in deluding the nations ...'.[16] This new eclecticism combined with the sophist argumentation of the Antiochene Church provided the Arian with 'a most powerful weapon to mislead or to embarrass his Catholic antagonist'.[17]

Newman believes the Arian heresy flourished in the imperial court which supported it, and that this corresponded to the liberalism in his Anglican Church. He observes that in the Arian crisis the Episcopal hierarchy was corrupted by the heresy while the laity kept the faith: 'The episcopate ... did not, as a class or order of men, play a good part in the troubles consequent upon the Council; and the laity did'.[18] In this work, Newman focuses on Athanasius and the faithful laity fighting against a corrupt episcopacy. According to Ferguson, 'such a myth prepared the way for Newman's work in the Oxford Movement, whose members saw themselves as leading the faithful laity to restore the church and to have a correct understanding of God over and against a corrupt Episcopal hierarchy'.[19] Newman understood history as a struggle between orthodoxy and heresy, and believed false belief will eventually be defeated by a small group of clerics together with the support of the laity. Williams rightly considers this work 'in large part, a tract in defence of what the early Oxford

---

15   Thomas Ferguson, 'The Enthralling Power: History and Heresy in John Henry Newman', *Anglican Theological Review* 85, no. 4 (Fall 2003), 650.

16   *Arians of the Fourth Century*,
http://www.newmanreader.org/works/arians/chapter1-4.html, 106.

17   Ibid., 113.

18   Ibid.,
http://www.newmanreader.org/works/arians/note5.html, 445.

19   Thomas Ferguson, 'The Enthralling Power: History and Heresy in John Henry Newman', *Anglican Theological Review* 85, no. 4 (Fall 2003),651.

Movement thought of as spiritual religion and spiritual authority. Such a picture naturally supports a high view of priestly authority, and a low view of the rights of secular power in the Church'.[20]

In *Arians,* Newman reveals the current state of the Church of England which was too weak to resist liberalism because it was divided, and the Anglican tradition with its reformation principles could not rescue her. His mission in the Oxford Movement, thus, was to educate and protect the laity from the enthralling heretical charms of liberalism. Ferguson argues that Newman's investigation into the Arian heresy operates from a hermeneutic which claimed heresy produced orthodoxy which would be the future Oxford Movement, and the heresy would be liberalism. Ferguson maintains that in *Arians*, Newman 'ushered the study of church history into modernity in England by contextualising it with the concerns of modernity, yet he did it with heresy as the backdrop'. This work reveals more about Newman's time than the fourth century.[21]

The Liberal Spirit in the Nineteenth Century

Religious liberalism in Newman's sense means that there is no positive truth in religion because of its anti-dogmatic nature. Newman's commitment to dogma in religion led him to oppose the attempt by the English Ultramontanes to interpret the doctrine of papal infallibility in the broadest scope, extending it to temporal matters. Newman thought that it was wrong of the Ultramontanes to claim as dogma what was only theological opinion.[22] Thus, Newman's opposition to liberalism

---

20   Rowan Williams, *Arius* (London: SCM Press, 2001), 5.
21   Thomas Ferguson, 'The Enthralling Power: History and Heresy in John Henry Newman', *Anglican Theological Review* 85, no. 4 (Fall 2003),659.
22   John F. Crosby, 'Newman's witness against the spirit of liberalism in religion' in *John Henry Newman* (Rome: Urbaniana University Press, 1981), 101.

works against both the liberal and conservative Catholics – he took a middle and balanced approach in his faith.

The 'imbecile optimism' which underlay the notion of liberalism was what Newman was opposing. This optimism he judged to be absurd on account of the doctrine of the Fall. This ignorance of the Fall has serious political implications – men saw the good in themselves and not evil, and wondered why certain parts of the social system failed. They eventually attributed their failure to lack of scientific knowledge rather than personal virtue.[23] Liberalism, then, can be seen as a kind of spirit or mood based on the mistaken idea that man is free from external will or guidance.

In *An Essay on the Development of Christian Doctrine*, Newman describes liberalism in terms of its basic tenets and attitudes although he does not use the word itself he characterises it as follows:

> That truth and falsehood in religion are but matter of opinion; that one doctrine is as good as another; that the Governor of the world does not intend that we should gain the truth; that there is no truth; that we are not more acceptable to God by believing this than by believing that; that no one is answerable for his opinions; that they are a matter of necessity or accident; that it is enough if we sincerely hold what we profess; that our merit lies in seeking, not in possessing; that it is a duty to follow what seems to us true, without a fear lest it should not be true; that it may be a gain to succeed, and can be no harm to fail; that we may take up and lay down opinions at pleasure; that belief belongs to the mere intellect, not to the heart also; that we may safely trust to ourselves in matters of Faith, and need no other guide,—this is the principle of philosophies and heresies, which is very weakness.[24]

Newman was against the kind of liberalism that identified Christianity with the humanistic ideals of the day. For him, religion was not merely a sense of propriety, civilization or education. He also rejected the idea of self-sufficiency of the natural man or the natural good, for religion, according to Newman, involved supernatural belief and di-

---

23　Terrence Kenny, *The Political Thought of John Henry Newman* (London: Longman, Green and Co., 1957), 129-130.

24　*An Essay on the Development of Christian Doctrine,* http://www.newmanreader.org/works/development/chapter8.html, 357-358.

vine grace. In his university lectures, he attacked the association of religion with sentiments rather than knowledge, and he defended the objectivity of dogma. Newman understood that a liberalism that involved the spread of anti-dogmatic attitude would lead to a subjective and rationalistic approach to religion, a denial that there are objective truths to be found in religion. For the liberals, theology resulted in opinion and should be discarded because it had vitiated true knowledge and indulged in useless controversies. Newman rejected this kind of thinking because this utilitarian approach was equally rationalistic in judging religion by secular criteria.[25]

In *Apologia,* liberalism is also defined as the anti-dogmatic principle which destroys the truths of Christianity by subjecting them to secular reason and denying their objective nature. Liberals believed that it is dishonest to believe without proof, impossible to believe without understanding, and that only those religious beliefs justified by reason are important. Newman, on the other hand, stressed the objective truth of the Christian faith which was not just an opinion or sentiment. Devotion could not be divorced from faith and religion could not be divorced from reason. Emotions or sentiments were no substitute for religion, and secular education or ethics could not replace the teaching authority of Christianity and the church. Liberalism, thus, was rationalism of the natural and fallen man. Newman did not object to secular principles or natural reason, but he was against applying or substituting them for those of Christianity.[26]

There were some liberals like Hampden who instead of treating church doctrines as sacred mysteries, would like 'to strip them of their mysteriousness and separate the practical from the impractical, the relevant from the irrelevant'.[27] Hampden believed scripture alone is the 'sole oracle' of revealed truth, not church or tradition.[28] He taught

25   Derek J. Holmes, 'J.H. Newman: History, Liberalism and the Dogmatic Principle', *Philosophical Studies* 23 (1975), 88.
26   Ibid., 89.
27   Francis McGrath, *John Henry Newman: Universal Revelation* (Mulgrave, Victoria: John Garratt Publishing, 1977), 54.
28   Ibid.

that religious doctrines are man-made, thus they are limited, open to rational scrutiny and can be held selectively without danger to salvation. Doctrines are just 'remnants' of a flawed theology and tradition carries no divine authority. Hampden insisted that we should respect the Fathers of the Church, but we are not obliged to accept them.[29] Thus, Newman and many others were outraged by Hampden's nomination to the Regius Professorship of Divinity in which he would be entrusted with the education of Anglican clergy. Newman reacted by publishing *Elucidation on Dr Hampden's Theological Statements* to expose Hampden's liberal principles.

Dogma and Revelation

Newman was distinguished by his vehement insistence on the importance of dogma which he believed was necessary since religious truth must be conveyed. This dogmatic stance was in fact his strong reaction to the subjective religious trend current in his time, partly influenced by the great Schleiermacher, which seemed to him to replace the objective truths of dogma by personal feelings and experience.[30] The logical sequence of liberalism when its subjectivism is played out is atheism, Newman concluded. If we reduce religious assertions to simply private judgement, this means that the strength of liberalism depends on the strength of opinions or sentiments.

Against this kind of liberalism, Newman stressed the role of conscience as the voice of God speaking to us, and that 'dogma adds to

29   Ibid.
30   Terrence Kenny, *The Political Thought of John Henry Newman* (London: Longman, Green and Co., 1957), 31. According to Professor Lai Pan Chiu, Newman's impression might be wrong, though common. See Lai Pan-chiu, 'Christian Theology in a Religiously Pluralistic Context: An Asian Revisit of Schleiermacher', *Journal of Asian and Asian American Theology* 4 (Spring 2001), 9-28.

conscience's inner testimony the social nature of genuine divine communication...'.[31] According to Edward Jeremy Miller, this understanding of revelation has a number of implications: first of all, dogma is 'a divine pedagogy', which means that God communicates to us his will and purposes. Thus, religion cannot be reduced to mere opinion or private judgement because it is God speaking to us, and we have to give our real assent. Second, dogma is symbolic and thus has an inner reality and an external manifestation, because God communicates to us in human forms. Although human words cannot fully express divine will, they are still necessary and important. The symbolic nature of dogma means that revelation must be expressed by human mode of communication no matter how imperfect it is. Third, dogma is necessary because God's message must enter into human history so that we, though overwhelmed by sins, can hear it clearly and live by it.[32]

These features of dogma formed the basis of Newman's ecclesiology. His understanding of dogma is wider and more fluid than what was generally accepted during his time, for he believed Jesus continues to communicate to us through the sacramental structure of the church. For Newman, the church as 'oracle of truth' is the 'ongoing symbol of revelation, ' and the church realises and makes concrete the message of Jesus.[33] Dogma is a statement expressing traditional dogmatic definitions such as 'Jesus is consubstantial with God the Father', which invites notional apprehension, or it may simply be a statement like 'Jesus died for me', giving us a concrete image. No matter how inadequate our language, the statement comes from real apprehension which is vital for religious devotion. Newman called this kind of statement or dogma the 'backbone of religion'.[34]

Naturally, Newman believed faith is not belief in proposition, but trust in a person, as scripture teaches us the importance of accepting

---

31 Edward Jeremy Miller, *John Henry Newman on the Idea of Church* (Shepherds-town, West Virginia: The Patmos Press, 1987), 18.

32 Ibid., 18-19.

33 Ibid., 19.

34 Quoted in Edward Jeremy Miller, *John Henry Newman on the Idea of Church* (Shepherdstown, West Virginia: The Patmos Press, 1987), 37.

Christ for our salvation. A religion based on dogmas can invite intellectualism as the evangelicals feared. However, Newman argued that religious feeling or devotion, 'vital religion', must be focused otherwise it will not last. Hence, religious imagination needs to have the backing of doctrines or propositions because our intellect needs words to work on.[35]

Dogmatic principle is important for Newman because of his conviction that Christianity is a revealed religion. Thus, in denying doctrine, liberalism denies revelation. For Newman, truth is 'thematic', especially in the case of revelation, because God speaks only when he has meant to say something that we should know. He writes:

> ... but that, after a Revelation is given, there is nothing to believe, nothing (to use an expressive Scripture word) to 'hold', to 'hold fast', that a message comes from God, and contains no subject-matter, or that, containing it (as it must do), it is not important to be received, and is not capable of being learned by any one who takes the proper means of learning it, that there is in it nothing such, that we may depend on our impression of it to be the true impression, may feel we have really gained something, and continue in one and one only opinion about it,—all this is so extravagant, that I really cannot enter into the state of mind of a person maintaining it. I think he is not aware what he is saying. Why should God speak, unless He meant to say something? Why should He say it, unless He meant us to hear? Why should we be made to hear if it mattered not whether we accepted it or no?[36]

Hence, in Newman's view, religion was about revelation, doctrines and creeds. It was not simply rational or philosophical because revelation was historical. Christianity for him was supernatural history revealed by God and thus it was objective and historical. Revelation was not a single complete message, but a developing teaching which culminated in the coming of Christ and was clarified gradually, and Newman looked towards an incorrupt Catholic fullness. He stood for a

---

35   Edward Jeremy Miller, *John Henry Newman on the Idea of Church* (Shepherdstown, West Virginia: The Patmos Press, 1987), 37.

36   'Holy Scripture in Its Relation to the Catholic Church' in *Discussions and Argument*,
      http://www.newmanreader.org/works/arguments/Scripture/lecture2.html, 130.

definite system of ecclesiastical faith that existed since the time of the apostles. It was a dogmatic system sanctioned in scripture, found in history and included the notion of revelation: 'The fact of a tradition of revealed truth was an elementary principle of Christianity'.[37] Thus, according to Newman, Christianity was a historical fact, an objective belief, an event, and not merely a personal affair. Genuine Christianity was not simply 'a hidden and isolated life, in the hearts of the elect' or mere information about God.[38]

Crosby observes that Christian revelation also gives rise to the anti-dogmatic bias of liberalism because of its ambiguity and the mystery it conveys.[39] Newman deals with this complexity in his tract on rationalism:

> No revelation can be complete and systematic, from the weakness of the human intellect; so far as it is not such, it is mysterious. When nothing is revealed, nothing is known, and there is nothing to contemplate or marvel at; but when something is revealed, and only something, for all cannot be, there are forthwith difficulties and perplexities. A Revelation is religious doctrine viewed on its illuminated side; a Mystery is the selfsame doctrine viewed on the side unilluminated. Thus Religious Truth is neither light nor darkness, but both together; it is like the dim view of a country seen in the twilight, with forms half extricated from the darkness, with broken lines, and isolated masses. Revelation, in this way of considering it, is not a revealed system, but consists of a number of detached and incomplete truths belonging to a vast system unrevealed, of doctrines and injunctions mysteriously connected together; that is, connected by unknown media, and bearing upon unknown portions of the system.[40]

37 *Essays Critical and Historical*,
    http://www.newmanreader.org/works/essays /volume1/ apostolical.html, 1:125.
38 *An Essay on the Development of the Christian Doctrine*,
    http://www. newmanreader.orgworks/development/introduction.html, 4.
39 John F. Crosby, 'Newman's witness against the spirit of liberalism in religion',
    in *John Henry Newman* (Rome: Urbaniana University Press, 1981), 104.
40 *Essays Critical and Historical*,
    http://www.newmanreader.org/works/essays/volume1/rationalism/setion1.html,
    1:41-42.

Newman understood that faith depended on testimony and revelation was a revealed system which must be taken as a whole. Religious truth was one and Christianity was a response to a total reality. The Deposit of Faith was not simply a list of propositions. The dogmatic principle was that supernatural truths written in human language must therefore be imperfect, but necessary and definite because they are divinely revealed. The words expressed the idea and the idea represented the fact. Dogma was the church's way of expressing its tenets which were to be held in faith.[41]

Dogmas were symbols of a divine fact which could not be adequately described or understood by a thousand prepositions. Newman defended the necessity of doctrinal definition, the importance of ecclesiastical authority and the exactness of orthodoxy. He also upheld the validity of creeds and dogmas, and recognized their limitations, but denied that such formulas varied with time and place.[42] In one of his sermons, he acknowledges that revelation involves a certain ignorance of some aspects and thus results in some intellectual difficulties:

> I consider that this mysteriousness is, as far as it proves any thing, a recommendation of the doctrine. I do not say that it is true, because it is mysterious; but that if it be true, it cannot help being mysterious. It would be strange, indeed, as has often been urged in argument, if any doctrine concerning God's infinite and eternal Nature were not mysterious. It would even be an objection to any professed doctrine concerning His Nature, if it were not mysterious. That the sacred doctrine, then, of the Trinity in Unity is mysterious, is no objection to it, but rather the contrary....[43]

Rationalism assumes that faith is sentimental, that man is self-sufficient, and miracles are impossible. Thus, reason endangered faith and showed the necessity of dogmas. Newman believed in eternal punishment because it had been divinely revealed and to deny it

41 Derek J. Holmes, 'J.H. Newman: History, Liberalism and the Dogmatic Principle', *Philosophical Studies* 23 (1975), 87.
42 Ibid., 88.
43 *Parochial and Plain Sermons*,
    http://www.newmanreader.org/works/parochial/volume6/sermon23.html, 6:333.

would compromise belief in other doctrines such as divine judgment and atonement. His attitude towards the dogmatic principle is succinctly described in these words: 'He has made history to be doctrine'.[44] Through the Incarnation, God revealed himself to man and the New Testament was the historical text of revelation. Faith for Newman means 'looking into Jesus' and he stressed that 'we are in danger, in this day, of insisting on neither of these as we ought; regarding all true and careful consideration of the Object of faith, as barren orthodoxy, technical subtlety…'.[45] Some people stressed the importance of a spiritual mind and heart ignoring dogmas as objective truths or articles of faith, but these human sentiments are the consequence of religion, not its main preoccupation.[46]

To view religion as primarily a human response would reduce the significance of the creed and emphasise moral qualities at the expense of belief. Such a subjective approach would play down the importance of the Incarnation as a revelation of God – this would result in the sentimentalism of paganism rather than knowledge of the Christian faith. Newman asserts that the 'Gospel Faith is a definite deposit – a treasure, common to all, one and the same in every age, conceived in set words, and such as admits of being received, preserved, transmitted'.[47] Doctrinal articles can be found throughout the New Testament and 'By the Faith is evidently meant, as St. Paul's words show, some definite doctrine; not a mere temper of mind or principle of action, much less, vaguely, the Christian cause'.[48] Newman did not believe that a doctrinal creed will degrade a real religious faith. Doctrinal formulas, although they are intellectual notions, are also propositions that ex-

44   Ibid.
      http://www.newmanreader.org/works/parochial/volume2/sermon19.html, II: 227.
45   Ibid.
      http://www.newmanreader.org/works/parochial/volume2/sermon14.html, II:153-154.
46   Derek J. Holmes, 'J.H. Newman: History, Liberalism and the Dogmatic Principle', *Philosophical Studies* 23 (1975), 90.
47   *Parochial and Plain Sermons*,
      http://www.newmanreader.org/works/parochial/volume2/sermon22.html, II: 256.
48   Ibid., II: 258.

press facts that are necessary just as language is necessary. To love God we need to know him, and religious devotion needs objects that are verbal propositions. Religious sentiments must always be guided by reason. Theology as a science might lack the life of religion, but religion cannot survive without theology.[49]

Private Judgment

This liberal trait that Newman found dangerous concerns the question of private of judgment in relation to religion. The ninth proposition of liberalism annexed to the 1865 edition of the *Apologia* reads: 'There is a right of Private Judgment: that is, there is no existing authority on earth competent to interfere with the liberty of individuals in reasoning and judging for themselves about the Bible and its contents, as they severally please'.[50] This usurpation of dogmatic religion is a main characteristic of liberalism in Newman's view:

> Now by Liberalism I mean false liberty of thought, or the exercise of thought upon matters, in which, from the constitution of the human mind, thought cannot be brought to any successful issue, and therefore is out of place. Among such matters are first principles of whatever kind; and of these the most sacred and momentous are especially to be reckoned the truths of Revelation. Liberalism then is the mistake of subjecting to human judgment those revealed doctrines which are in their nature beyond and independent of it, and of claiming to determine on intrinsic grounds the truth and value of propositions which rest for their reception simply on the external authority of the Divine Word.[51]

---

49   *An Essay in Aid of a Grammar of Assent,*
     http://www.newmanreader.org/works/grammar/chapter5-1.html#section1,120-121.
50   *Apologia pro Vita Sua,*
     http://www.newmanreader.org/works/apologia65/chapter4-2.html, 295.
51   Ibid., 288.

As early as 1829, Newman was beginning to sense the pervasive liberal spirit in society in its insistence on the right of private judgment. In the past, people accepted the teaching of the clergy, but now they tried to judge for themselves. Christianity is not opposed to free inquiry, but Newman believes a spirit is at work against Christianity, 'a spirit which tends to over throw doctrine, as if the fruit of bigotry and discipline – as if the instrument of priest craft. All parties seem to acknowledge that the stream of opinions is setting against the Church'.[52]

In 1832, Newman told his congregation that when dogma is rejected as religious truth, men fall back on themselves, and religion becomes 'a mere civilization'.[53] He was convinced the great majority of people are not capable of using their own judgment to arrive at religious truth. The tenth proposition of liberalism states that human being has the right to profess and teach what seems to be true according to his private conscience, but this right makes the individual responsible for the truth of his religion.[54] Eventually it becomes a duty and a burden. Newman understood that this insistence on private judgment in religious matters led many people of his time to treat faith as subjective, the reality of which exists only in the mind of the individual. However, this does not mean that private judgment has no place in the life of the faithful. Newman argues that once Christians have submitted to orthodox doctrine, they may exercise private judgment in their choice of life, in matters of duty – secular or religious.[55]

Hence, his support for private judgment in matters of personal duty is connected to his distrust of private judgment in matters of doctrine. For him, the correct use of private judgment presumed an act of submission to dogma. This goes against the nineteenth century attitude

---

52 Quoted in Thomas Vargish, *Newman: The Contemplation of Mind* (Oxford: Clarendon Press: 1970), 79.

53 *Parochial and Plain Sermons*, http://www.newmanreader.org/works/parochial/volume1/sermon3.html, 1:30.

54 *Apologia pro Vita Sua*, http://www.newmanreader.org/works/apologia65/notea.html, 295.

55 Thomas Vargish, *Newman: The Contemplation of Mind* (Oxford: Clarendon Press: 1970), 86-87.

towards the right of private judgment, and Newman labelled it as false liberty of thought, the error of subjecting Christian dogma to human reason. English attitude towards private judgment includes the right to determine what is false and true in Christianity - the burden of proof is on the individual Christian who is responsible for the accuracy of his own religious convictions. Eventually, the liberal spirit in society treats religion not as a body of objective truths, but as the way by which persons define themselves in the universe, and it becomes merely the satisfaction of needs and not the glorification of God.[56] In his *Apologia*, Newman believes this liberal spirit threatens to shake the foundation of society and he describes the liberal as the 'Anti-Christ exalting himself above the yoke of religion and law. The spirit of lawlessness came in with the Reformation, and Liberalism is its offspring'.[57]

Reformation and the Bible

Although the Bible alone, in the sense of private interpretation, is a possible source of revelation, Newman did not believe it will work this way. The Reformers upheld the Bible as the main source of authority, replacing a teaching church with a teaching book. But Newman believed Christians need an enduring and decisive voice to guide them.[58] Private judgment in religious matters cannot work, he argued, because piety needs the backing of doctrines or dogmas, and the Bible was never meant to be a judge for doctrinal disputes. The principle of private interpretation of the Bible has divided Christianity into many

---

56   Ibid., 88.
57   Quoted in Thomas Vargish, *Newman: The Contemplation of Mind* (Oxford: Clarendon Press: 1970), 88.
58   *An Essay on the Development of Christian Doctrine*, http://www.newmanreader.org/works/development/chapter2.html, 87.

denominations and sects. In a letter to an unknown correspondent, September 10, 1875, Newman writes:

> 'The sacred text was never intended to teach doctrine, that if we would learn doctrine, we must have recourse to the formularies of the Church, for instance to the Catechism and to the Creeds'. And is not this abundantly clear? ... Why do Wesleyan schools turn out Wesleyan pupils as their resulting process, Congregationalists Congregational youths, and the Church of England schools Episcopalians? If the Bible teaches doctrine clearly, why do some readers arise from it Trinitarians, others Unitarians, and others Calvinists? Why do not all readers of the Bible at least agree in what are fundamentals, what not? I do not know what is *meant* by saying that Scripture is adapted, is intended, to teach the very truth of revelation, if in matter of fact it does not do so.[59]

The Bible arose from the apostolic church and must be read within a tradition. Although Newman did not have an advanced knowledge of the origin of the scripture, he had an innate sense of the relationship between the Bible and tradition, and he recognised that Protestants upholding private biblical interpretation must also read scripture within their own tradition and confession, as did Catholics like himself. The church, thus, is the only real successor to the teaching of the apostles. Private judgment in Bible reading cannot provide the definite doctrines required for devotion. Revelation occurred within a community when God spoke to his people, and therefore, it requires correct interpretation as the community enters into history and faces new challenges.[60]

Universal education, progress of civilization or even the reliance on the Bible cannot check the onslaught of secularism and atheism as Newman explains: 'A book, after all, cannot make a stand against the wild living intellect of man, and in this day it begins to testify, as regards its own structure and contents, to the power of that universal solvent, which is so successfully acting upon religious establish-

---

59 Quoted in Edward Jeremy Miller, *John Henry Newman on the Idea of Church* (Shepherdstown, West Virginia: The Patmos Press, 1987), 39.

60 Edward Jeremy Miller, *John Henry Newman on the Idea of Church* (Shepherdstown, West Virginia: The Patmos Press, 1987), 39-40.

ments'. Only an institution that possesses 'a direct, immediate, active, and prompt means of withstanding the difficulty' can check this 'wild living intellect'.[61] This institution must be divinely appointed and invested with the power of infallibility in religious matters. It should be able to define its limits and to discern if new developments are in accord with the Deposit of Faith. This institution would preserve the spiritual truth on which our human knowledge and society is based. Such an institution, Newman concluded, must be the Catholic Church, which alone is capable of protecting the authoritative source of spiritual truth revealed by God to man.

The sixth lecture of the series, 'On the Abuse of Private Judgment', again accepts that the Bible is a difficult book to read, and Newman scorns the popular view that 'every Christian has the right of making up his mind for himself what he is to believe, from personal and private study of the Scriptures'. He is against the 'preposterous' notion that 'every individual Christian, rich and poor, learned and unlearned, young and old, in order to have an intelligent faith, must have formally examined, deliberated, and passed sentence upon the meaning of Scripture'.[62] Newman admits that ordinary folk with their own prejudices and weaknesses may acquire religious impressions and practical guidance from scripture, but he does not think that they are capable of formulating sound doctrines from it.

Against Liberal Rationalism

Most of Newman's criticisms of his society come in the form of an attack on liberalism which he associated with rationalism or human

---

61   *Apologia pro Vita Sua,*
     http://www.newmanreader.org/works/ apologia65 /chapter5.html, 245.
62   *Lectures on the Prophetical Office of the Church,* 'Via Media 1',
     http://www.newmanreader.org/ works/viamedia/volume1/lecture6.html, 145.

reasoning unaided by the light of Christian dogma. In the *Apologia*, he traces this scepticism in his adult life:

> The Liberalism which gives a colour to society now, is very different from that character of thought which bore the name thirty or forty years ago. Now it is scarcely a party; it is the educated lay world. When I was young, I knew the word first as giving name to a periodical, set up by Lord Byron and others. Now, as then, I have no sympathy with the philosophy of Byron. Afterwards, Liberalism was the badge of a theological school, of a dry and repulsive character, not very dangerous in itself, though dangerous as opening the door to evils which it did not itself either anticipate or comprehend. At present it is nothing else than that deep, plausible scepticism, of which I spoke above, as being the development of human reason, as practically exercised by the natural man.[63]

He regarded the reforming and rational spirit that was pervading the Anglican Church in the enactment of the Bill for Catholic Emancipation as a liberal spirit, 'one of the signs of the time ... encroachment of Philosophism and Indifferentism in the Church'.[64] Later he saw the spirit of liberal Protestantism as the great evil that threatened Anglicanism, and thus, the battle was not with Catholicism, but rationalism. When the Anglican bishops rejected his Tract 90, which to Newman meant the only possible Catholic interpretation of the Thirty-nine Articles, he thought the church must have become dangerously liberal. He was at this time developing the idea of a fundamental dialectic in which Catholicism was the thesis and liberalism the anti-thesis. By 1839, Newman decided that Protestantism lay between Catholic truth and rationalism.[65]

According to Holmes, Newman's attitude towards the theological implication of liberalism was consistent as evident in his major discussion of 1839 and his definition written in 1887:

---

63 *Apologia pro Vita Sua*,
    http://www.newmanreader.org/works/apologia65/chapter5.html, 261.
64 Quoted in Thomas Vargish, *Newman: The Contemplation of Mind* (Oxford: Clarendon Press: 1970), 74.
65 Ibid., 75.

Liberalism is the *development* of rationalism. It views faith as a mere natural gift, the like and consequence of reason – the moral sense; and by reason and the moral sense [the rationalist] estimates it and measures its objects. He soon comes to be satisfied with other men though they ignore faith and its objects, provided they recognise reason and the moral sense.[66]

In Tract 73, Newman asserts that 'Rationalism is a certain abuse of Reason; that is, a use of it for purposes for which it never was intended, and is unfitted'.[67] Faith believes in testimony, but rationalism subjected revelation to reason. Newman accepted the facts that reason can help to investigate some religious truths and that it was not rationalistic to try to interpret revelation. But rationalism attempted to judge revelation by secular criteria, as its basic assumptions was that belief demanded empirical proof. Newman was against this because this approach made human reason, rather than God, the central point in revelation. Religion became a subjective understanding and not a belief in an objective truth beyond reason. In the rationalistic approach faith is limited to understanding 'the history of a series of divine actions',[68] but for Newman Christianity means submission to God's authority, and the notion of revelation contains a certain mystery. This personal understanding of a subjective revelation is called a 'manifestation'. The human mind cannot fully understand the entire revelation: 'the revelation was one aspect of truth, the mystery was the other 'hidden' side'.[69]

---

66   Quoted in Derek J. Holmes, 'J.H. Newman: History, Liberalism and the Dogmatic Principle', *Philosophical Studies* 23 (1975), 91.

67   *Essays Critical and Historical*, http://www.newmanreader.org/works/essays/volume1/rationalism/section1.html , I: 31. See also Colin Gunton, 'Newman's Dialectic Dogma and Reason in the Seventy-Third *Tract for the Times*' in *Newman after a Hundred Years*, edited by Ian Ker and Alan G. Hill (Oxford: Clarendon Press, 1990), 309-322.

67   Derek J. Holmes, 'J.H. Newman: History, Liberalism and the Dogmatic Principle', *Philosophical Studies* 23 (1975), 91.

68   Derek J. Holmes, 'J.H. Newman: History, Liberalism and the Dogmatic Principle', *Philosophical Studies* 23 (1975), 91.

69   Ibid.

The doctrine of the atonement, for example, is part of a mystery and cannot be subjected to rational explanation. If we consider this doctrine primarily in its practical results, and presume to understand it fully, we reduce its significance as the revelation of a divine truth. Hence, the doctrine of atonement cannot be reduced to a mere manifestation of the love of Christ and the mercy of God. Newman insisted that we must accept revelation in all its entirety and keep its formulas strictly because revelation is expressed through words or actions and cannot exist apart from them.[70] The rationalist tried to make revelation in a system that can be understood by all, and presented it 'when thus mutilated, as affording a remarkable evidence of the truth of the Bible, an evidence level to the reason, and superseding the testimony of the Apostles'.[71] Newman insisted that to consider any aspect as central to revelation was to assume that we have a full understanding of it, and thus, fall into the danger of excluding details that did not conform to our human understanding.[72]

The liberal as a rationalist cannot endure the mystery of religion because he needs to hold on to the object of his belief by clear understanding, and thus he refuses to take any interest in things that are beyond his comprehension. The effect of this kind of religious attitude is to dissolve doctrine because of its mystery that is beyond reason.[73] For example, the liberal rationalist cannot accept that the sacrificial death of one man can change the course of history and affect the fundamental relationship between God and man. This mystery he rejects as primitive and prefers to view it as an expression of God's love for us, and to give us an example of what loving our neighbour means. The sacrificial nature and atonement of Christ's death is denied by the lib-

---

70 Ibid.
71 *Essays Critical and Historical*,
    http://www.newmanreader.org/works/essays/volume1/rationalism/section1.html,
    1:48.
72 Derek J. Holmes, 'J.H. Newman: History, Liberalism and the Dogmatic Principle', *Philosophical Studies* 23 (1975), 92.
73 John F. Crosby, 'Newman's witness against the spirit of liberalism in religion', in *John Henry Newman* (Rome: Urbaniana University Press, 1981), 104.

eral rationalist. This is an example of 'the all-corroding, all-dissolving scepticism of the intellect in religious inquiries' that Newman expresses in his *Apologia.*[74]

Newman, on the other hand, exults in the mystery of Christian revelation implied in Christian doctrine:

> Therefore, so far from considering the Truths of the Gospel as a burden, because they are beyond our understanding, we shall rather welcome them and exult in them, nay, and feel an antecedent stirring of heart towards them, for the very reason that they are above us.[75]

He brings to light the mystery in religion in the following passage:

> Thus was it, we are told, from everlasting;—before the heavens and the earth were made, before man fell or Angels rebelled, before the sons of God were formed in the morning of creation, yea, before there were Seraphim to veil their faces before Him and cry 'Holy', He existed without ministers, without attendants, without court and kingdom, without manifested glory, without any thing but Himself; He His own Temple, His own infinite rest, His own supreme bliss, from eternity. O wonderful mystery! O the depth of His majesty! O deep things which the Spirit only knoweth! Wonderful and strange to creatures who grovel on this earth, as we, that He, the All-powerful, the All-wise, the All-good, the All-glorious, should for an eternity, for years without end, or rather, apart from time, which is but one of His creatures, that He should have dwelt without those through whom He might be powerful, in whom He might be wise, towards whom He might be good, by whom He might be glorified. O wonderful, that all His deep and infinite attributes should have been without manifestation! ... He, the All-powerful God, rested from eternity, and did not work ....[76]

74   Quoted in John F. Crosby, 'Newman's witness against the spirit of liberalism in religion', in *John Henry Newman* (Rome: Urbaniana University Press, 1981), 105.

75   *Parochial and Plain Sermons,*
       http://www.newmanreader.org/works/parochial/volume2/ sermon18.html, II: 207.

76   *Parochial and Plain Sermons,*
       http://www.newmanreader.org/works/parochial/volume6/ sermon25.html,
       VI:364-365.

Newman's profound sense of the mystery in Christian revelation is one of the characteristic marks of his spirituality. According to Crosby, Newman adores mystery even before he reached the limits of his understanding; St Thomas Aquinas and St Anselm used their reason to the fullest in understanding the Christian faith, but in Newman we find the opposite tendency. Crosby asserts that Newman 'in exulting in the mysteries of nature and grace ... lives out a religiosity which is in direct opposition to the rationalism of liberalism'.[77] While delighting in the mystery of religion, Newman does not find doctrine irrelevant as the liberal does, but actually finds it to be a mystery. In his sermons, he writes:

> What are those deep hidden reasons why Christ went and the Spirit came? Marvellous and glorious, beyond our understanding! Let us worship in silence; meanwhile, let us jealously maintain this, and every other portion of our Creed, lest, by dropping jot or tittle, we suffer the truths concealed therein to escape from us.[78]

Liberalism implies that religion should fall under the domain of reason – we must be able to understand it fully and it must satisfy and fulfil our needs. Hence, the atonement of Christ is understood purely as God's love for us – the focus is on human being alone. It is offensive to the liberal that the atonement is seen as the satisfaction of divine justice and the glorification of God. Hence the liberal does not accept the Athanasian Creed which deals mostly with the inner life of the Trinity and has little to say about man and his salvation. The liberal also cannot accept the doctrine of eternal punishment, which Newman always defends because it goes against the liberal emphasis on human fulfilment. Crosby asserts that 'the very idea of ascribing importance to doctrine [of atonement] at all is resented [by the liberals] on anthropocentric presuppositions, because taking doctrine seriously inevitably

---

77 John F. Crosby, 'Newman's witness against the spirit of liberalism in religion', in *John Henry Newman* (Rome: Urbaniana University Press, 1981), 107.

78 *Parochial and Plain Sermons*,
http://www.newmanreader.org/works/ parochial/volume2/ sermon18.html, II: 213.

leads to divisions among men, and religion is thought to have no right to interfere with human solidarity'.[79]

Liberalism tends to discard mystery from religion, shifting the emphasis from God to man. Rationalism in liberalism demands clear knowledge about the divine so that human aspiration can find its fulfilment. Newman believed this anthropocentric concern of liberalism would pave the way for atheism.[80] In one of his sermons, Newman points out the danger of this kind of self-centred concern of man in the rationalist rejection of mystery in religion which might lead to apostasy:

> As great then as is the difference between hanging upon the thought of God and resting in ourselves, lifting up the heart to God and bringing all things in heaven and earth down to ourselves, exalting God and exalting reason, measuring things by God's power and measuring them by our own ignorance, so great is the difference between him who believes in the Christian mysteries and him who does not.[81]

Newman is not only committed to the dogmatic principle in religion, he is also filled with authentic piety. He teaches us that we not only dwell on what God has done for us, but also on him as He is – the inner life of God. And if a person only centres exclusively on God as redeemer and not on God as He is, he is in danger of moving towards liberalism.[82] On Trinity Sunday, Newman preaches:

> The Annunciation, the birth of Christ, His death on the Cross, His Resurrection, the descent of the Holy Ghost, are all mysteries; but we celebrate them, not on this account, but for the blessings which we gain from them. But today we celebrate, not an act of God's mercy towards us, but, forgetting ourselves, and looking only upon Him, we reverently and awfully, yet joyfully, extol the wonders,

79   John F. Crosby, 'Newman's witness against the spirit of liberalism in religion', in *John Henry Newman* (Rome: Urbaniana University Press, 1981), 108.
80   Ibid.
81   *Parochial and Plain Sermons*,
      http://www.newmanreader.org/works/parochial/volume4/ sermon19.html, IV: 293.
82   John F. Crosby, 'Newman's witness against the spirit of liberalism in religion', in *John Henry Newman* (Rome: Urbaniana University Press, 1981), 110.

not of His works, but of His own Nature. We lift up heart and eyes towards Him, and speak of what He is in Himself. We dare to speak of His everlasting and infinite Essence; we directly contemplate a mystery, the deep unfathomable mystery of the Trinity in Unity.[83]

As seen from the above, authentic religion means that our focus should be on God and not how God can fulfil our needs – it is the spirit of adoration. Liberalism, however, seeks to make man the criteria of all things, using God, as it were, as an instrument for greater human fulfilment.

Newman also found great attraction in the Athanasian Creed with its stress on the trinitarian doctrine. The mystery of the trinitarian doctrine was not a burden for him; it was not 'an intrusion of Greek metaphysics into Christian devotion' as the liberal would like to say.[84] In *An Essay in Aid of a Grammar of Assent*, Newman says the Athanasian Creed is 'the most simple, the most devotional formulary to which Christianity has given birth' and 'it is a psalm or hymn of praise, of confession, and of profound self-prostrating homage, parallel to the canticles of the elect in the Apocalypse'.[85] There is also a passage in which Newman anticipates the vision of God in eternity and seeks to live out the dogmatic principle:

After the fever of life ... at length comes death, at length the White Throne of God, at length the Beatific Vision. After restlessness comes rest, peace, joy;— our eternal portion, if we be worthy; —the sight of the Blessed Three, the Holy One; the Three that bear witness in heaven; in light unapproachable; in glory without spot or blemish; in power without 'variableness, or shadow of turning'. The Father God, the Son God, and the Holy Ghost God; the Father Lord, the Son Lord, and the Holy Ghost Lord; the Father uncreate, the Son uncreate, and the Holy Ghost uncreate; the Father incomprehensible, the Son incomprehensi-

---

83   *Parochial and Plain Sermons,*
      http://www.newmanreader.org/works/parochial/volume6/ sermon23.html, VI:
      327-328.
84   John F. Crosby, 'Newman's witness against the spirit of liberalism in religion'
      in *John Henry Newman* (Rome: Urbaniana University Press, 1981), 111.
85   *An Essay in Aid of a Grammar of Assent,*
      http://www.newmanreader.org/works/grammar/chapter5-2.html, 133.

ble, and the Holy Ghost incomprehensible. For there is one Person of the Father, another of the Son, and another of the Holy Ghost; and such as the Father is, such is the Son, and such is the Holy Ghost; and yet there are not three Gods, nor three Lords, nor three incomprehensibles, nor three uncreated; but one God, one Lord, one uncreated, and one incomprehensible.[86]

Reason and Religion

In spite of his opposition to liberal Anglicanism, Newman accepts reason in theological investigation provided it respects its limits. For example, it is not rationalism to ascertain what matters are 'attainable by reason, and what are not'. It is also not rationalism to investigate into the truths of natural religion when there is no expressed revelation. Likewise in Newman's view, it is not rationalism to 'investigate the meaning of its declarations, and to interpret its language' when a genuine revelation is recognised.[87]

Newman also points out that those who love moral and religious truths may use their intellectual power in the service of religion for 'belief in revealed religion is not inconsistent with the highest gifts and acquirements of mind, and that men even of the strongest and highest intellect have been Christians'.[88] He also declares that Christianity forms the whole man which includes reason, feelings, affections, imagination and conscience.[89] Newman does not find fault with the

86   *Parochial and Plain Sermons,*
     http://www.newmanreader.org/works/parochial/volume6/ sermon25.html, VI: 369-370.

87   Quoted in Francis McGrath, *John Henry Newman: Universal Revelation* (Mulgrave, Victoria : John Garratt Publishing, 1977), 63.

88   *Parochial and Plain Sermons,*
     http://www.newmanreader.org/works/parochial/volume8/ sermon13.html, VIII:190.

89   Ibid.,

operation of reason *per se,* for reason is good as far as it goes. But reason cannot provide much information about God's nature and hence cannot lead one to virtuous action. In one of his sermons, Newman turns explicitly to the role of reason in religious inquiry. It is clear from the text that he is not against reason in and of itself for he states that:

> Clear-sighted as reason is on other subjects, and trustworthy as a guide, still in questions connected with our duty to God and man it is very unskilful and equivocating. After all, it barely reaches the same great truths which are authoritatively set forth by Conscience and by Scripture; and if it be used in religious inquiries, without reference to these divinely-sanctioned informants, the probability is, it will miss the Truth altogether.[90]

Newman also does not deny the use of reason in religious enquiries, but his concern is to ascertain the true role of the intellect in the question of faith.[91] 'Religiously-trained reason' is described by him as the 'educated conscience' or 'rightly directed Reason'[92], and religion involves truths of which the moral sense (i.e. conscience) is the legitimate judge; and we may 'freely cultivate the Reason in all its noble functions'.[93] Although Newman upholds the importance of moral dispositions, it does not mean leaving reason out of consideration. In fact, he acknowledges that the movement to faith is a kind of implicit reasoning: 'So alert is the instinctive power of an educated conscience, that by some secret faculty, and without any intelligible reasoning process, it seems to detect moral truth wherever it lies hid'.[94]

---

http://www.newmanreader.org/works/parochial/volume6/sermon24.html, VI:353.
90   Ibid.,
http://www.newmanreader.org/works/parochial/volume1/sermon17.html, I: 219.
91   *Oxford University Sermons,*
http://www.newmanreader.org/works/oxford/sermon4.html, 63.
92   Ibid.,
http://www.newmanreader.org/works/oxford/sermon4.html, 66.
93   Ibid.,73.
94   Ibid.,66.

In a sermon on June 29, 1840, Newman made a distinction between 'implicit' and 'explicit' reason – the former implies an unconscious process by which the mind reaches its conclusion, and the latter is the logical development of thought through an analysis of the former. Implicit reasoning is a rational process and judges a thing as a living, feeling, knowing, and willing subject. Newman believed formal logic could never capture the complex workings of the human mind in search of religious truth[95] and 'Faith, then, though in all cases a reasonable process, is not necessarily founded on investigation, argument or proof; these processes being but the explicit form which the reasoning takes in the case of particular minds'.[96] According to Merrigan, Newman made the distinction between implicit and explicit reason to claim that that reason was 'a much more personal, and a much richer process than the prevailing philosophy allowed'.[97]

Newman was disillusioned with rationalism and saw it as a threat to Christianity. In his parochial and university sermons, he reasserted the moral dimension of faith, and actually equated faith with moral conduct. John Elbert argues that Newman had 'a tendency to reduce faith to a practical principle' and 'went so far as to identify faith with conscientiousness, righteousness or holiness – in short, with that saving faith known in Catholic theology as *fides formata*'.[98] His years at Oriel College enabled him to realise the limits of scientific reason, and the importance of moral dispositions and endeavour. However, this in no way suggests that he was becoming illiberal.

In the final analysis, Newman accepts the fact that faith is a rational act as shown in his *An Essay in Aid of a Grammar of Assent*. Newman's orientation and dogmatic faith prevented him from adopting a rationalistic and logical outlook in religion. At the same time, he

---

95   Ibid.,
     http://www.newmanreader.org/works/oxford/sermon13.html, 258-259.
96   Ibid., 262.
97   Terrence Merrigan, 'Newman's Oriel experience: its significance for his life and thought', *Bijdragen* 47, no. 2 (1986),208.
98   Quoted in Terrence Merrigan, 'Newman's Oriel experience: its significance for his life and thought', *Bijdragen* 47, no. 2 (1986),209.

was actually attracted to the liberal spirit in 1827 where the tendency was to place reason before faith and knowledge before devotion.[99] This is understandable, for Newman in *Apologia* speaks of the Noetics with affection for they had made a deep impression on him even though he did not agree with everything they taught. He felt at home in Oriel, and in spite of himself, he did enjoy the company of the Noetics who provided him with a stimulating environment to forge his own thought. However, his association with Keble and Froude and his study of the Patristic literature eventually made him change his mind. Newman was impressed with the moral dispositions of both these men, and through them re-discovered holiness as the root of Christian life, and that the truth is reached not 'by mere intellectual ability or learned study', but must instead 'be sought by the whole man, his faculties purified by obedience to the light of conscience'.[100] Although this is considered the highlight of his 'Oriel Experience', it must be stressed again that it is by no means a complete rejection of the liberal spirit prevailing in the university.

Liberal Theology

In *Essays Critical and Historical*, Newman insists we cannot judge revelation in terms of morality alone because not all revealed doctrine has direct influence on moral character. He asserts that Erskine had occasionally made statements denying the truth of doctrine that did not have moral implications. But for Newman, revealed doctrines are

---

99   Terrence Merrigan, 'Newman's Oriel experience: its significance for his life and thought', *Bijdragen* 47, no. 2 (1986), 203.

100   Quoted in Terrence Merrigan, 'Newman's Oriel experience: its significance for his life and thought', *Bijdragen* 47, no. 2 (1986), 203.

the 'objects of faith' and 'motives to conduct'.[101] He believes in the mystery of religion as religious fact, whereas Erskine restricted revelation to 'a series of historical works conveying a representation of the moral character of God'.[102]

Erskine and Abbott, both liberal theologians, considered the Gospel as merely a collection of facts – the application of rationalism to revelation.[103] Both considered the Gospel history as a *manifestation* of God. Erskine admitted the existence of supernatural phenomena such as the Incarnation, whereas Abbott confined himself to the humanity of Christ and saw the Gospel in human terms. Abbott regarded the New Testament as a human record, looking at the external aspect of revelation and displaying a 'Socinian bias in his view of the saviour'.[104] Abbott disregarded the real divinity of Christ – the Incarnation was for Abbott just a moral manifestation of God in the person of Christ – and thus, the value of atonement was not in expiation by the moral effect of Christ's death. Such an approach, Newman believed, placed too much stress on the external events through which divine truths were revealed.[105]

Newman considered Thomas Chalmers' influential interpretation of Christianity as coming close to liberalism. He condemned this teaching because it claimed that God was a God of justice, but later

---

101 *Essays Critical and Historical,*
     http://www.newmanreader.org/works/essays/volume1/rationalism/ section2.html, I: 61.
102 Ibid., I:70.
103 Ibid.,
     http://www.newmanreader.org/works/essays/volume1/rationalism/section3.html I: 72-95.
104 Ibid., I: 90.
105 Derek J. Holmes, 'J.H. Newman: History, Liberalism and the Dogmatic Principle', *Philosophical Studies* 23 (1975), 92-93. Colin Gunton acknowledges that Newman is justified in his criticism of Erskine and Abbott; 'A Christianity dominated by thoughts of relevance only advertises its own irrelevance'. See Colin Gunton, 'Newman's Dialectic Dogma and Reason in the Seventy-Third *Tract for the Times*' in *Newman after a Hundred Years*, edited by Ian Ker and Alan G. Hill (Oxford: Clarendon Press, 1990), 311, 314.

became only a God of love because justice had been satisfied. This comes close to liberal thinking because it taught that the fear of God was an imperfect Jewish sentiment which was not relevant in modern times. Chalmers described the moral attribute of God as essentially benevolence, in line with the positions of most liberal theologians like Sir James Macintosh who were opposed to the Athanasian Creed.

Thus Chalmers looked only at the practical implications of doctrinal belief and not at the biblical testimony. This may result in denying the Trinity or the Incarnation as necessary for salvation, and stress only the atonement. Newman's defence of the dogmatic principle was based on his understanding of revealed religion as historical – he was convinced of the historical nature of Christianity. At the same time, he believed any attempt to interpret the history of Christ in human or secular terms was an example of rationalism, and thus erroneous. This inevitably would lead to theological error or even heresy like Socinianism which denied the divinity of Christ.[106] Newman's understanding of Christianity as a historical event is centred on his discussion of the work of a liberal Anglican, Henry Hart Milman. In *History of Christianity*, Milman argues that the success of Christianity over Judaism had resulted in it losing its original purity, but Newman believes such a claim would destroy Christianity. Christian doctrines would be destroyed if we were to subject them to reason and trace their origins to a human source, and revelation would only have introduced a 'quality in our moral life' and not an objective teaching; the consequence would be that 'Christianity will melt away in our hands like snow'.[107] It will be seen merely as an influential historical event based on error and not on religious truth.

In 'Milman's view of Christianity', Milman applies the principles of historical criticism to scripture, and in his theological writings there was a pronounced liberal attitude. The underlying principle was the notion of intellectual progress. Holmes explains:

---

106 Ibid., 93.
107 *Essays Critical and Historical*,
     http://www.newmanreader.org/works/essays/volume2 /milman2.html, II: 242.

Nations developed from an imaginative to a reflective state and this explained the pattern of thought at any particular time. The literal interpretation of Scripture was seen in the light of the 'accommodation' of religion or revelation to the progress of civilization and was simply one aspect of divine condescension. Any imperfections in the Old Testament were natural and inevitable at the particular stage of development, while Christianity would necessarily reflect these same qualities in an imaginative or mythical age.[108]

Liberal Anglicans were aware that religion could not be fully accommodated with rationalism. The theory of accommodation and the notion of progress involved a certain relativism, and Newman found it hard to understand how this could be compatible with the notion of revelation. Milman's work, particularly the *History of the Jews*, written in a 'hasty thoughtless irreverent spirit', was infected with a 'supercilious spirit of liberalism' that encouraged him to seem 'philosophical and above the world'[109] to show that an enlightened clergyman could still believe. This approach alarmed Newman, who saw it as dangerous because it ignored the element of divine revelation. According to Holmes, he was extremely suspicious of the historians of the new school, although he did learn a lot from them.[110]

In *The Idea of a University*, Newman refers to the *History of the Jews* regarding the application of secular criteria to divine revelation: 'I must conclude that he [Milman] was simply betrayed into a false step by the treacherous fascination of what is called the Philosophy of History, which is good in its place, but can scarcely be applied in cases where the Almighty has superseded the natural laws of society and history'.[111] In Lecture 3 of *Discussions and Arguments*, 'Structure of the Bible, antecedently considered', Newman describes the action of divine providence as the result 'of a long history of change and

---

108   Derek J. Holmes, 'J.H. Newman: History, Liberalism and the Dogmatic Principle', *Philosophical Studies* 23 (1975), 94.
109   Quoted in Derek J. Holmes, 'J.H. Newman: History, Liberalism and the Dogmatic Principle', *Philosophical Studies* 23 (1975), 94.
110   Ibid., 95.
111   *The Idea of a University*,
       http://www.newmanreader.org/works/idea/discourse4.html. 85.

chance', and the 'casual writings of the Apostles' became 'a complete canon of saving faith'.[112]

Not every part of scripture is religious, but it actually made use of contemporary sources such as pagan philosophies. Pagan customs could be used without contradicting the Christian faith. In *Parochial and Plain Sermons*, Newman writes,

> Now the system of this world depends, in a way unknown to us, both on God's Providence and on human agency. Every event, every course of action, has two faces; it is divine and perfect, and it belongs to man and is marked with his sin... it is a peculiarity of Holy Scripture to represent the world on its providential side; ascribing all that happens in it to Him who rules and directs it, as it moves along, tracing events to His sole agency, or viewing them only so far forth as He acts in them ... As common is it for Scripture to consider Dispensations, not in their actual state, but as His agency would mould them, and so far as it really does succeed in moulding them...In other words, Scripture more commonly speaks of the Divine *design* and *substantial work*, than of the *measure* of fulfilment which it receives at this time or that....[113]

The Jewish people had a distinctive way of worshipping the true God, but their political principles or historical events were identical with those of the surrounding nations. Externally Judaism seemed like another Eastern religion, but with different internal principles. Thus, the external form of Judaism was natural, but God had specially inspired it with his own spirit. This is also true for Christianity, which is a divine treasure in an earthly vessel. God always used human means to achieve his divine purpose.[114] Newman understood revelation as the completion of natural religion. The religion of the New Testament has a certain universality in it, and different aspects of all religions where truth was found seemed to originate from a common source. Religion was primarily a worship of God and this implied common elements in

112 *Discussions and Arguments,*
      http://www.newmanreader.org/works/ arguments/Scripture/lecture3.html, 150.
113 *Parochial and Plain Sermons,*
      http://www.newmanreader.org/works/parochial/volume2/ sermon8.html, II: 82.
114 Derek J. Holmes, 'J.H. Newman: History, Liberalism and the Dogmatic Principle', *Philosophical Studies* 23 (1975), 96.

all religious faiths which included liturgical ceremonies and practices as a means of organizing the system of belief.[115]

Newman was prepared to accept historical evidence against a theological opinion, but he believed that theories did not have the same force. Evidence could disprove, whereas theories can only show probabilities in particular cases, and could also be opposed by other probabilities.[116] He believed that to study only the human aspects of revelation would result in liberalism or even heresy, and so would modification of theological facts by subjecting them to reason. It is also wrong to accept or reject parts of scripture according to our personal preferences. Newman admitted it was possible to argue history against prophecy or the finding of conscience against doctrine, but revelation professed to reveal what was unknown. And thus, 'it was impossible to subject revealed doctrines to preconceived notions or arbitrary moral theories'.[117]

Newman was against the principles on which Milman based his writing, and his final conclusion on Milman's *History of Christianity* was that it contained 'so much to shock people, that there is comparatively little to injure'.[118] The question is how to write sacred or church history without compromising on theological belief – how to reconcile historical methods with divine providence? Newman believed it was wrong to subject revelation to human reason, and it was also equally wrong to subject historical facts to faith and disregard historical evidence. Newman never denied that there was a common ground between scared and secular history, or that sacred history could be discussed according to historical facts. But we cannot treat sacred history on purely historical ground – this would result in theological error.

115 *Parochial and Plain Sermons,*
     http://www.newmanreader.org/works/parochial/volume5/sermon12.html,   V: 169-177.
116 Derek J. Holmes, 'J.H. Newman: History, Liberalism and the Dogmatic Principle', *Philosophical Studies* 23 (1975), 99-100.
117 Ibid., 100.
118 *Essays Critical and Historical,*
     http://www.newmanreader.org/works/essays/volume2/milman2.html, II: 247.

Besides, natural explanations of events in scripture did not necessarily destroy their divine origin.[119]

Newman was not concerned about Milman's assertion that Christianity appropriates material from other religions, but he was alarmed by Milman's 'arbitrary reduction of the miraculous or supernatural elements in the New Testament, his rejection of all private miracles such as visions of angels'. According to Wright, 'this for Newman is an unholy compromise, an abandonment of tradition, an ignoble attempt to 'reconcile the faith of eighteen centuries' with 'the infidelity of the nineteenth'.'[120]

The Fear and Love of God

Newman's attack on liberalism is due not only to its anti-dogmatic principle, but also to its fundamental attitude towards God and man – that liberalism is anthropocentric. Newman speaks of holy fear towards God, a disposition to have the right relation to religious truth, to venerate it. This attitude of fearing God is unacceptable to the liberals.[121] But Newman teaches that Christians must not only love God, but fear Him, not with a slavish dread, but with a reverential awe. Just as fear becomes slavish if not coupled with love, so love becomes superficial if it is isolated from fear. According to Crosby, the teaching of holy fear permeates Newman's sermons – it becomes a distinctive mark of his spirituality.[122] Newman is critical of the religion of his day

---

119   Derek J. Holmes, 'J.H. Newman: History, Liberalism and the Dogmatic Principle', *Philosophical Studies* 23 (1975), 102.

120   T.R. Wright, 'Newman on the Bible: A *Via Media* to Postmodernity' in *Newman and the Word*, edited by Terrence Merrigan and Ian T. Ker (Louvain: Peeters Press, 2000), 242.

121   John F. Crosby, 'Newman's witness against the spirit of liberalism in religion', in *John Henry Newman* (Rome: Urbaniana University Press, 1981), 112.

122   Ibid., 113.

which is devoid of fear, and this forms part of his protest against the spirit of liberalism that resents reverential fear in religion. Liberalism teaches that fear is a slavish thing for man and his needs should be the measure of religion. But Newman's understanding of holy fear is part of his dogmatic stand, and he believes that 'the man who fears God will venerate the truth about God'.[123]

Religious zeal is also connected to the dogmatic principle in that it looks towards God as the measure of all things. This piety becomes the veneration of religious truth because we display zeal when we uphold religious doctrine.[124] Newman teaches that St. John the Apostle, while abounding in love, also showed much zeal in questions of truth:

> He loved the brethren, but he 'loved them in the Truth'. [3 John 1.]... He loved the world so wisely, that he preached the Truth in it; yet, if men rejected it, he did not love them so inordinately as to forget the supremacy of the Truth, as the Word of Him who is above all.[125]

The spirit of zeal is particularly strong in Newman's Oxford sermons and tracts, and in the poems (*Verses on Various Occasions*) he wrote during his sea journey in 1832-33. In his poems, Newman is filled with burning zeal for the house of God and for dogma that reveals the truth of God. According to Crosby, this teaching of zeal is part of his witness against the spirit of liberalism, a spirit which sees zeal as intolerance, fanaticism, and a lack of love. The preaching of zeal for God's honour is almost non-existent in present-day churches. This is understandable because we live in pluralistic society, and it is important to stress tolerance and unity among believers and non-believers. However, Crosby believes this is a defect in Catholic spirituality, and Newman's teaching can help us to attain a more balanced and complete Catholic spirituality.[126]

---

123 Ibid., 114.
124 Ibid., 115.
125 *Parochial and Plain Sermons*,
        http://www.newmanreader.org/works/parochial/volume2/sermon23.html,II:285-286.
126 Ibid., 117.

Deformation of Natural and Revealed Religion

Newman also speaks of the spirit of liberalism as a 'certain deformation of revealed religion' and also as a 'deformed natural religion'.[127] God as the centre of all things belongs naturally to both revealed and natural religions, and the shift of gravity to make man the measure of all things is destructive to both types of religions. Holy fear and zeal also form part of revealed and natural religions, and liberalism aversion to them corrupts both.[128] Liberalism in natural religion involves a certain distortion of conscience, and for Newman, conscience is 'the creative principle of religion'.[129] This distortion of conscience in liberal thinking lies in its denial of God as the supreme lawgiver and judge in choosing between good and evil, and this means conscience loses it religious significance. Liberalism tends to view conscience as a kind of self-respect, personal integrity and concern for one's genuineness – we think of ourselves as fools rather than as sinners when we act immorally.[130]

In the *An Essay in Aid of a Grammar of Assent*, Newman states that our consciences have been perverted in this way, and hence, natural religion falls apart because men begin to think that:

> moral evil and physical ... [are] nothing more than imperfections of a parallel nature ... that there is a progress of the human race which tends to the annihilation of moral evil; that knowledge is virtue, and vice is ignorance; that sin is a bugbear, not a reality; that the Creator does not punish except in the sense of correcting; that vengeance in Him would of necessity be vindictiveness... that prayer to Him is a superstition; that the fear of Him is unmanly; that sorrow for

---

127 Ibid.
128 Ibid.
129 *An Essay in Aid of a Grammar of Assent*,
http://www.newmanreader.org/works/grammar/chapter5-1.html#section1,110.
130 John F. Crosby, 'Newman's witness against the spirit of liberalism in religion', in *John Henry Newman* (Rome: Urbaniana University Press, 1981), 118.

sin is slavish and abject; that the only intelligible worship of Him is to act well our part in the world, and the only sensible repentance to do better in future ....[131]

Religion of Civilization

The liberalism that Newman was opposing is aptly described by Robert Pattison as the 'worship of civilization at the expense of faith'.[132] The spirit of liberalism, in its scepticism of the intellectual in religious matters, affects natural as well as revealed religion. This was the prevailing opinion in the age and culture in which Newman lived, which was considered 'civilised'. Liberalism is a deformation of religion, but not everyone is susceptible to it. It affects the educated class mainly because liberalism presupposes a 'cultivation of the intellect'.[133] It made its way into Oxford University through the reformers at the beginning of the nineteenth century. Newman did not, however, think the intellectual life will necessarily lead to liberalism, but there is a tendency towards it because of human frailty. Newman's idea of a Catholic university shows how intellectual life can be led without succumbing to the dangers of liberalism.[134]

Intellectuals tend to live in ivory towers, and are more at home in liberalism. They cannot take the severity in religion that calls for sacrifice and atonement, and they cannot understand people zealous for God's glory. Newman depicts this kind of gentlemen and their instinctive liberalism in *The Idea of a University*. He believes there is a unity

---

131 *An Essay in Aid of a Grammar of Assent,*
     http://www.newmanreader.org/works/grammar/chapter10-2.html, 416.
132 Robert Pattison, *The Great Dissent* (Oxford: Oxford University Press, 1991), 43.
133 Quoted in John F. Crosby, 'Newman's witness against the spirit of liberalism in religion', in *John Henry Newman* (Rome: Urbaniana University Press, 1981), 119.
134 John F. Crosby, 'Newman's witness against the spirit of liberalism in religion', in *John Henry Newman* (Rome: Urbaniana University Press, 1981), 119.

between our intellect and conscience. When it comes to religious truth, our heart and mind form a unity in order to discern the truth. If our hearts are not pure, we cannot discern the truth of religion. It is not the same for other secular disciplines. One can be a good scientist and an immoral person at the same time. Newman asserts that when the intellectual powers are divorced from moral nature, we cannot apprehend the truth:

> Now it should not surprise us when men of acute and powerful understandings more or less reject the Gospel, for this reason, that the Christian revelation addresses itself to our hearts, to our love of truth and goodness, our fear of sinning, and our desire to gain God's favour; and quickness, sagacity, depth of thought, strength of mind, power of comprehension, perception of the beautiful, power of language, and the like, though they are excellent gifts, are clearly quite of a different kind from these spiritual excellences - a man may have the one without having the other ... Who would ever argue that a man could see because he could hear, or run with the swift because he had 'the tongue of the learned'? [Isa. l. 4.] These gifts are different in kind. ... as all the highest spiritual excellence, humility, firmness, patience, would never enable a man to read an unknown tongue, or to enter into the depths of science, so all the most brilliant mental endowments, wit, or imagination, or penetration, or depth, will never of themselves make us wise in religion.[135]

Intellectual Life and Liberal Thinking

Newman believes that in cultivating the intellectual life, one tends to neglect the conversion of the heart which is more difficult to attain. Hence, the intellectual development becomes one-sided, and the person approaches religious matters as mere intellectual problems to be solved. He enquires only with his mind and not with his whole being. Newman protests against this kind of intellectualism when he asserts

---

135 *Parochial and Plain Sermons,*
   http://www.newmanreader.org/works/parochial/volume8/sermon13.html, VIII: 188-189.

in his *Essay on the Development of Christian Doctrine* that 'the search for truth is not the gratification of curiosity ... its attainment has nothing of the excitement of a discovery ... the mind is below truth, not above it, and is bound, not to descant upon it, but to venerate it'.[136] This intellectualism which Newman speaks never wants to reach final conclusion, it merely wants to seek and not to possess, and thus, it is anti-dogmatic, and 'seeks its natural level in liberalism'.[137]

Liberalism is regarded as a child of certain intellectualism and does not possess solid ground in religious experience; it is only capable of theorising about religion. In his early sermons, Newman also speaks about the impotency and inability of liberalism to cope with difficulties in spite of its optimism regarding human nature:

> But, fairly as this superficial view of human nature answers in peaceful times; speciously as it may argue, innocently as it may experimentalise, in the rare and short-lived intervals of a nation's tranquillity; yet, let persecution or tribulation arise, and forthwith its imbecility is discovered. It is but a theory; it cannot cope with difficulties; it imparts no strength or loftiness of mind; it gains no influence over others. It is at once shattered and crushed in the stern conflict of good and evil; disowned, or rather overlooked, by the combatants on either side, and vanishing, no one knows how or whither.[138]

In contrast to the weakness of liberalism, he speaks about the strength of dogmatic principle: 'Dogmatism was in teaching, what confession was in act'.[139] This commitment to revealed truth is manifested by the lives of the martyrs. Christianity was distinguishable from the sects which surrounded the early church as Newman writes:

136 *Essay on the Development of Christian Doctrine,*
   http://www.newmanreader. org/works/ development/chapter8.html, 357.
137 John F. Crosby, 'Newman's witness against the spirit of liberalism in religion', in *John Henry Newman* (Rome: Urbaniana University Press, 1981), 123.
138 *Oxford University Sermons,*
   http://www.newmanreader.org/works/oxford/sermon6.html, 103.
139 *Essay on the Development of Christian Doctrine,*
   http://www.newmanreader. org/works/ development/chapter8.html, 359.

These sects had no stay or consistence … and had Christianity been as they, it might have resolved into them; but it had that hold of the truth which gave its teaching a gravity, a directness, a consistency, a sternness, and a force, to which its rivals for the most part were strangers. It could not call evil good, or good evil, because it discerned the difference between them; it could not make light of what was so solemn, or desert what was so solid. Hence, in the collision, it broke in pieces its antagonists, and divided the spoils.[140]

Newman protested against liberalism by his writings and life with great acuteness and forcefulness because he was afraid that the liberal spirit in religion would eventually lead to atheism. He believed that church authority and tradition would be a good defence against this onslaught of secularization.[141] So far we have examined Newman's criticism of liberalism that promoted relativism in faith and morals, denied positive truths and dogmatic principles in religion. In the next chapter we will discuss the liberal legacy of Newman by examining his writings on various issues.

---

140 Ibid.,
     http://www.newmanreader.org/ works/development/chapter8.html, 358-359.
141 See Mark S. Burrows, 'A historical reconsideration of Newman and liberalism: Newman and Mivart on science and the church', *Scottish Journal of Theology* 40, no. 3 (1987), 401 – 417.

Chapter 4

The Liberal Ideas of Newman

As an Anglican, Newman portrayed himself as the relentless foe of 'the Liberalism of the day' in his *Apologia*. He wanted to expose the damage done to Christianity by the liberals who disregarded tradition. As one of the leaders of the Oxford Movement, he attempted to promote the wisdom of the Church Fathers and opposed any novelty in the church. Newman was afraid modernity and new ideas would destroy Christianity in society if liberalism began to take root, which in fact it already had. However, after his conversion to Catholicism in 1845, he appeared to tone down his attack on liberalism and became sympathetic to Catholic liberals without changing his own basic disposition. Critical of modernism and its hostility to faith, he was also critical of the conservatism in the Roman Catholic Church with its excessive control.

In Oxford, he stressed the pastoral role of the college tutor; as founding rector of a Catholic University in Dublin, he emphasised intellectual freedom; and in *The Idea of a University*, he called for liberal education. There was also a shift in his ecclesiology: in the Church of England, Newman stressed Episcopal authority and responsibility, and in the Church of Rome, he stressed participation, defending the interests of an educated laity with his essay in the *Rambler* of July 1859, 'On Consulting the Faithful'. Misner rightly observes that this shift is not so much a change in outlook as an effort to achieve a balance. Although Newman fought against the anti-dogmatic principle in liberalism, he also understood the intellectual deficiencies of Catholicism in the nineteenth century and its over dependency on received doctrine.[1]

As a convert, Newman could not do much in theology, but in the field of higher education, he had hoped the bishops would not oppose Catholics attending universities at Oxford or Cambridge because the church needed an educated laity to take their place in public life as did their Protestant peers. Unfortunately, Cardinal Wiseman and the Congregation of the Propaganda in Rome, influenced by Cardinal Manning and Wilfrid Ward, began to oppose Catholics attending old Protestant Universities. When the *Syllabus of Errors* came out in 1865 in the newspaper, Newman acknowledged that 'we are certainly under a tyranny'.[2] However, his sense of obedience, of facing trials as a purification, and of solidarity with the ordinary laity and clergy was strong. He did not go against ecclesiastical authority no matter how mistaken the church might have been.[3]

Misner says it was Lord Acton who requested Newman to consider enlarging the discussion on the problem of honesty and truthfulness in the church, including the freedom of scholars to present their findings to others.[4] Hence, in the *Apologia*, Newman added this: 'The said authority may be accidentally supported by a violent ultra party, which exalts opinions into dogmas, and has it principally at heart to destroy every school of thought but its own'.[5] In a private letter to his bishop at the First Vatican Council, a letter that later became public knowledge early in 1870, Newman expressed his concern over the rush to promulgate papal infallibility because it was a doctrine that

1   Paul Misner, 'The "liberal" legacy of John Henry Newman' in *Newman and the Modernists* (Lanham, Md: University Press of America, 1985), 7.

2   Quoted in Paul Misner, 'The "liberal" legacy of John Henry Newman' in *Newman and the Modernists* (Lanham, Md: University Press of America, 1985), 7.

3   Paul Misner, 'The "liberal" legacy of John Henry Newman' in *Newman and the Modernists* (Lanham, Md: University Press of America, 1985), 7-8.

4   Ibid., 8.

5   *Apologia pro Vita Sua*,
     http://www.newmanreader.org/works/apologia65 /chapter5.html, 260.

was hard to define accurately, although he did believe it was true.[6] The effort to push the definition of papal infallibility through the council without proper discussion was scandalous, and Newman regarded Ultramontane party members like Manning, Ward and Cardinal Herbert Vaughan as conspirators in 'an aggressive insolent faction'.[7]

The Council formulated the Pope's infallibility only as an exercise in special and rare circumstances of 'that infallibility with which the divine Redeemer wished to endow his Church', and this infallibility was only for the purpose of defining doctrine on faith and morals. Newman understood this as limiting infallible teaching to matters of revelation, but the Ultramontanes proceeded to interpret the dogmatic constitution of July 18, 1870 as broadly as possible, which resulted in doctrinal confusion. Newman then published his *Letter to the Duke of Norfolk* in 1875, in which he 'defended the doctrinal import of the new dogma of papal infallibility from the exaggerations of Manning on the one side by refuting the parallel exaggerations of Gladstone on the other'.[8] This work demonstrates Newman's display of learning and was a huge success in winning young thinkers and future writers like Ward and Baron Friedrich von Hügel.[9]

Newman also represented cultural liberalism in the same way as Friedrich Schlegel did – both of them were hostile to popular education. For Schlegel, liberalism was a cultured state, and the illiberal

---

6   In his letters, between 1866 and 1868, Newman expressed this issue of papal infallibility in the following: 'I have ever thought it likely to be true, never thought it was certain'. 'On the whole, then, I hold it, but I should account it no sin if, on grounds of reason, I doubted it'. 'I hold the Pope's Infallibility, not as dogma, but as a theological opinion; that is, not as a certainty, but as a probability'. 'I have only an opinion (not faith) that the Pope is infallible'. Quoted in Francis A. Sullivan, SJ, and 'Newman on Infallibility' in *Newman after a Hundred Years*, edited by Ian Ker and Alan G. Hill (Oxford: Clarendon Press, 1990), 430.

7   Quoted in Paul Misner, 'The "liberal" legacy of John Henry Newman' in *Newman and the Modernists* (Lanham, Md: University Press of America, 1985), 9.

8   Ibid.,10.

9   Ibid.

man was a philistine and 'adorer of mediocrity'.[10] Newman shared similar views with Schlegel regarding the need for a liberal education which find full expression in *The Idea of a University*.[11]

Edward Norman argues that Newman was 'not in any ordinary sense a liberal Catholic', but in his opposition to the temporal power of the papacy; and in his limited interpretation of papal infallibility, he was closer to the liberal Catholics, although his reasoning was different from theirs.[12] Newman also believed Christianity and knowledge were compatible, and that a proper understanding of the relationship between faith and culture was important to gain an insight into religious truth. Liberal Catholics and modernists also sought to reconcile Catholicism and secular knowledge, but they were not aware of the inherent values in those structures. They were critical of the past but not the present. Newman, however, understood that change was inevitable, and that dogma can provide a standard to assess the transformation that was occurring in both the secular and religious spheres.[13] He resisted liberalism only when it held that there is no positive truth in religion and one creed is as good as another, as we have seen earlier.

Modernity and Modernism

Born in the nineteenth century, Newman had experienced modernity which was seen as a threat to traditional Catholic faith in his time; modernity includes individualism which we take for granted now. Martin Luther stood for individualism when he claimed that the individual has the free authority to interpret scripture and to develop a

---

10   Terrence Kenny, *The Political Thought of John Henry Newman* (London: Longman, Green and Co., 1957), 164.
11   Ibid.
12   Edward Norman, *Roman Catholicism in England* (Oxford: Oxford University Press, 1985), 99.
13   Ibid.

personal relationship with God. Ronald Burke reminds us that such an emphasis on rights and responsibilities was not part of medieval culture.[14] Modernity also includes a new appreciation for cultural specificity and a growing recognition that people from different cultures dealt with things differently. According to Burke 'these differences gave some persons a self-reflective recognition of the interdependence of thought and culture. Not only are cultures slowly shaped by human thought; in subtle and encompassing ways, human thought itself is largely shaped by the thinker's surrounding culture'.[15] Newman grew up in a particular modern culture, was educated at Oxford, and raised as an Anglican; and hence he was in no sense a traditional Catholic priest trained in scholasticism. As a result, he was able to deal with the issue of doctrinal development in the church which involved an understanding of modernity and history as a process.

'Modernism' was a term used by Pius X and the Roman Curia to describe certain liberal, anti-scholastic and historico-critical forms of thoughts in the Catholic Church between 1890 and 1914. According to Richard McBrien, modernism implies that 'there can be no real continuity between dogma and the reality they presume to describe', and a dogma is more 'a rule of conduct than a rule of faith'.[16] As we have seen, Newman was against this kind of modernism. McBrien also acknowledges that the modernists must be commended for their efforts to bring some historical realism to the interpretation of Christian faith.[17] In this aspect, some of Newman's writings were quite correctly interpreted as having a modernist outlook.

George Tyrrell considered Newman the father of modernism, because, innocent of scholasticism and formed in the tradition of British empiricism, he wrote his religious ideas in the 'living thought-forms of his culture'. Tyrrell also pointed out that Newman was like

---

14   Ronald R. Burke, 'Newman, Lindbeck and Models of Doctrine' in Michael E. Allsopp and Ronald R. Burke ed., *John Henry Newman: Theology and Reform* (New York: Garland Publishing, Inc., 1992), 20.

15   Ibid., 21.

16   Richard P. McBrien, *Catholicism* (New York: HarperCollins Publishers, 1994), 49.

17   Ibid.

Thomas Aquinas, who applied the teaching of Aristotle in his work, because he was an 'essentially liberal-minded' spirit and had an 'elastic sympathy with contemporary culture'. Thomas had successfully translated the deposit of faith into a marvellous dogmatic system based on the current philosophical and theological thought form of his day. The problem is that scholasticism, instead of imitating Thomas' method – as Newman had done – slavishly took his system, but failed to be imbibed with his inquiring spirit.[18]

Tyrrell argued that 'Newman's theology formulates certain subjective immanent impressions or ideas analogous to sense impressions which are realities of experience by which notions and inferences can be criticised'.[19] This in principle is 'Liberal Theology' and what Tyrrell meant by 'liberal' is that Newman's theology was 'non-Scholastic'. The term 'liberal' was replaced by 'modernism' in the early twentieth century.[20] Tyrrell insisted that it is important to distinguish between the content of Newman's thought and his philosophical method, for he applied the liberal method to justify his conservative stand. Newman's mind was liberal but his temperament and sentiments were conservative.[21]

Newman had found the Roman theology mechanical and impersonal. Gabriel Daly argues that Newman's rejection of Paley's rationalism is actually a rejection of Roman fundamental theology, especially its approach to the theology of revelation which is rationalistic.[22] In *An Essay in Aid of a Grammar of Assent*, Newman says he did

---

18   David G. Schultenover, 'George Tyrrell: Devout Disciple of Newman', in *John Henry Newman: Theology and Reform*, edited by Michael E. Allsopp and Ronald R. Burke (New York: Garland Publishing, Inc., 1992), 69-70.

19   Quoted in Gabriel Daly, 'Newman, Divine Revelations, and the Catholic Modernists', in *Newman and the Word*, edited by Terrence Merrigan and Ian T. Ker (Louvain: Peeters Press, 2000), 50.

20   Gabriel Daly, 'Newman, Divine Revelations, and the Catholic Modernists', in *Newman and the Word*, edited by Terrence Merrigan and Ian T. Ker (Louvain: Peeters Press, 2000), 53.

21   Ibid., 55-56.

22   Ibid., 56.

not wish to be converted by a smart syllogism or to convert others by overcoming their reason without touching their hearts:

> If I am asked to use Paley's argument for my own conversion, I say plainly I do not want to be converted by a smart syllogism; if I am asked to convert others by it, I say plainly I do not care to overcome their reason without touching their hearts...And how after all, is a man better for Christianity, who has never felt the need of it or the desire? On the other hand, if he has longed for a revelation to enlighten him and to cleanse his heart, why may he not use, in his inquiries after it, that just and reasonable anticipation of its probability, which such longing has opened the way to his entertaining?[23]

Newman's most influential work, *Essay on the Development of Christian Doctrine*, views doctrinal development in accordance with historical and material influences – revealed truth is transmitted through human agency and subjected to historical processes. He was convinced that all life is change and that 'men cannot become external to their own involvement with the stuff of reality'.[24] Development shows continuities, and Catholic teachings like Marian devotions not found in antiquity are actually fruits of the process. According to Norman, Newman stood in the English tradition of Empirical thinking:

> [Newman's] idea of development valued tradition yet placed it upon a shifting basis; it recognized the relativity of human investments in what were incorrectly regarded as immutable expression of truth while it saw an essential deposit of revealed knowledge at the centre; it appreciated the corruption of institutions while it found permanency in a universal perception of authentic apostolic doctrine.[25]

In this work, Newman applies the general philosophy of movement that was dominating western thought at the end of the eighteenth century and beginning of the nineteenth century. This theory of move-

---

23 *An Essay in Aid of a Grammar of Assent*,
    http://www.newmanreader.org/works/grammar/chapter10-2.html, 425.
24 Edward Norman, *Roman Catholicism in England* (Oxford: Oxford University Press, 1985), 100.
25 Ibid.

ment and development culminated in the philosophy of Hegel and Darwin's theory of evolution. Newman argues that although the Church of Rome appeared to have added many things which seemed like excesses and idolatries, she in fact had not corrupted the Gospel. He accepts the notions of process and evolution, and applies them to the continuity and history of the Catholic Church.

According to Quinn, *Essay on the Development of Christian Doctrine* is also a refutation of all that integralism stands for – 'a cast of mind and outlook that is in some ways more pernicious than doctrinal indifference or heterodoxy'.[26] Like the fundamentalist, the integralist tries to absolutise everything, select papal and church teachings in order to support their rigidity of mind. Integralism believes that faith, the church and doctrine, coming from the past, must remain unchanged. It must admit of no diversity of expression and no new insights. Clearly, Newman could not accept this narrow-minded ideology that blocks communion, freedom and understanding. Thus, he attempts to demonstrate that the content of revelation is akin to the 'idea' Christianity impressed on the imagination.

The notion of a 'living idea' requires a concept far wider and richer than what was used in the nineteenth century. Although revelation was definitely and completely given from the beginning, Newman also held that it was present in some way in the original idea impressed on the imagination. In this work, he says the apostles knew all the truth of theology without words and later the theologians began to formulate and develop them through argument. In other words, Christian scholars translate the apostles' experience into words and concepts.

Newman in the tradition of modernism approached the theology of revelation by emphasising experience, especially moral experience, and the important role played by the imagination in the apprehension and interpretation of experience. Daly claims that these issues are still important today and 'the appeal to experience in liberal theology of all

---

26 John Raphael Quinn, 'Orthodoxy as opposed to fundamentalism, theological liberalism, and integralism', *New Oxford Review* 58 (May 1991), 22.

kinds, including that of the Modernists, was intended as a corrective to essentialism and extrinsicism'.[27] Daly also asserts that 'the appeal of both Newman and the Modernists to wordless and concept-less mental experience as the initial moment in the reception of revelation is open to challenge from a variety of postmodernists; but challenge, as Newman pointed out, is one of the ways through which great ideas are developed'.[28]

A Modernist Text: *Grammar of Assent*

It was Newman, Tyrrell told Ward in 1893, who would 'unbarbarise us and enable us to pour Catholic truth from the scholastic into the modern mould without losing a drop in the transfer', and thus Tyrrell would set out 'to prosecute [his] analysis of the *Grammar of Assent*'.[29] In *Essay in aid of a Grammar of Assent*, Newman showed that he had more in common with the modernists than the anti-modernists in that he discussed the assent of faith as a growth in imaginative responsiveness. Part of modernism implies that religious language can only approximate realities to which assent is given; it cannot replicate it exactly. In *Grammar of Assent*, we see the modernist's demand answered – the 'distinction between what is revealed and how it is described, defined, and spoken of'.[30] Hence, in spite of their differences,

27 Gabriel Daly, 'Newman, Divine Revelations, and the Catholic Modernists', in *Newman and the Word*, edited by Terrence Merrigan and Ian T. Ker (Louvain: Peeters Press, 2000), 53.

28 Ibid.

29 Quoted in David G. Schultenover, 'George Tyrrell: Devout Disciple of Newman', in *John Henry Newman: Theology and Reform*, edited by Michael E. Allsopp and Ronald R. Burke (New York: Garland Publishing, Inc., 1992), 70.

30 Quoted in Paul Misner, 'The "liberal" legacy of John Henry Newman' in *Newman and the Modernists* (Lanham, Md: University Press of America, 1985), 15.

Newman had more in common with the Modernists than the Anti-Modernists.

In the first part of *Grammar of Assent*, he justifies the principle of dogma as a pattern of ordinary mental consideration which functions as 'real assent' as opposed to 'notional assent'. These realities are made known to us through the power of imagination, and no amount of reasoning could convince us that they are mere probabilities. The element of trust does not make it less certain. In the life of faith, both the educated and uneducated give a real assent through devotion to a personal God. The role of moral conscience helps us acknowledge the reality of the divine being, and dogma aids in our devotion to God.

In Part II of *Grammar of Assent*, Newman shows that we can believe what we cannot absolutely prove. In everyday living, we give unconditional assent to facts, truths and moral assessment of situations without proof or validity. Rationalistic or scientific evidences account for very little in our human knowledge, and they are certainly not the most important part. We normally act or respond through instinct or intuition. Newman calls this process of arriving at certitude in practical matters 'informal inference', an operation that is more fundamental than formal logic:

> ... that the processes of reasoning which legitimately lead to assent, to action, to certitude, are in fact too multiform, subtle, omnigenous, too implicit, to allow of being measured by rule, ... they are after all personal, - verbal argumentation being useful only in subordination to a higher logic.[31]

Rules for scientific investigation do not apply to everyday affairs or matters for personal decisions in conscience. The 'illative sense' is simply this spontaneous process of reasoning in concrete matters – one learns how to do through practice and experience. Newman also stresses that probability is the guide of life. The converging and accumulative probabilities to certitude through informal inference is lik-

---

31 *An Essay in Aid of a Grammar of Assent*, http://www.newmanreader.org/works/grammar/chapter8-2.html, 303.

ened to a cable made up of many weak strands or to a polygon expanding into the enclosing circle.[32] His writings on faith, reason and personal conscience provide an alternative approach to the neoscholastic apologetic with its emphasis on intellectually probative demonstrations of the existence of God. Newman took Locke seriously and brought together the questions in religious epistemology.[33]

Liberal Catholicism

Liberal Catholicism was a new phenomenon among English Catholics in the nineteenth century. In 1858, its two leading representatives, Lord Acton and Richard Simpson, were in charge of a periodical called the *Rambler*, which under their direction, soon came into conflict with the ecclesiastical authorities because it was permeated by a form of liberalism.[34] Cardinal Wiseman warned his priests of the *Rambler*'s 'treatment of persons or things deemed sacred, its gazing over the edges of the most perilous abysses of error, and its habitual preferences of uncatholic to Catholic instincts, tendencies, and motive'.[35] In reply, Acton wrote that 'principles of religion, government, and science, are in harmony, always and absolutely; but their interests are not. And though all other interests must yield to those of religion, no principle can succumb to any interest. A political law or a scientific truth may be perilous to the morals or the faith of individuals, but it cannot on this ground be resisted by the church ... A discovery may

32 Paul Misner, 'The "liberal" legacy of John Henry Newman' in *Newman and the Modernists* (Lanham, Md: University Press of America, 1985), 15.

33 Ibid., 16.

34 K Theodore Hoppen, 'W. G. Ward and liberal Catholicism', *Journal of Ecclesiastical History* 23, no. 4 (October 1972), 331.

35 Quoted in K Theodore Hoppen, 'W. G. Ward and liberal Catholicism', *Journal of Ecclesiastical History* 23, no. 4 (October 1972), 339.

be made in science which will shake the faith of thousands; yet religion cannot refute it or object to it'.[36]

The period of these reviews, 1858-1864, was a time of great struggle between liberal Catholicism and Ultramontanism. Newman was clearly on the side of the liberal Catholics, although he might not agree with the way they acted or expressed themselves. He sympathised with many of Acton's views and realised that the church must take note of new scientific theories. He also strongly supported the liberal Catholics in their demand for an intellectual awakening among the Catholics and insisted that the modern state must not force a particular religion or its teachings on its members.[37] A supporter of the secular state, Newman was prepared to accept religious plurality. Far in advance of his time, he stressed the role of the laity in the church in his article, 'On Consulting the Faithful in Matters of Doctrine'. He was also a thinker of much greater originality and depth than either Acton or Ward, and adopted a more balanced approach in religious matters and ecclesiastical policies.

Catholics were beginning to open up to the values of the modern world such as self-determination and scientific spirit before the publication of Pius IX's *Syllabus of Errors* in 1864. 'Liberal Catholics' were led by a desire to bridge the gap between an obsolete clerical culture that no longer served the church's mission in the world and the intellectual, social and political challenges of the day. The church was successful in keeping the nineteenth century at bay due to the development of Ultramontanism (papalism) which was originally an anti-Gallican movement. However, Catholics like Félicité de Lamennais, Antonio Rosmini, Henri-Dominique Lacordaire, the abbé Maret,

---

36   Ibid.

37   Terrence Kenny, *The Political Thought of John Henry Newman* (London: Longman, Green and Co., 1957), 18. Norman, however, argues that Newman had 'unclear affinity' with the Liberal Catholics on various issues. Newman was never really a Liberal Catholic himself and his empirical outlook in politics was an insignificant part of his general outlook. See Edward Norman, 'Newman's Social and Political Thinking', in *Newman after a Hundred Years*, edited by Ian Ker and Alan G. Hill (Oxford: Clarendon Press, 1990), 168.

Charles Montalembert and Lord Acton, who had chosen to accommodate to the realities of the modern age were considered 'Liberal'. And as I have mentioned earlier, Newman was 'a figure head of the reformed-minded Catholics in the early twentieth century'.[38]

Liberal Education

In *The Idea of a University*, Newman defended the idea that 'cultivation of mind is surely worth pursuing for its own sake' and that just such cultivation is a university's proper object:

> When, then, we speak of the communication of Knowledge as being Education, we thereby really imply that that Knowledge is a state or condition of mind; and since cultivation of mind is surely worth seeking for its own sake, we are thus brought once more to the conclusion, which the word 'Liberal' and the word 'Philosophy' have already suggested, that there is a Knowledge, which is desirable, though nothing come of it, as being of itself a treasure, and a sufficient remuneration of years of labour.[39]

This is liberalism in the Aristotelian sense - the cultivation of knowledge for its own sake, acquiring intellectual satisfaction and possessing truth for its own sake. This is the dignity and value of liberal knowledge that Newman tried to promote in this work: 'that Liberal Education, viewed in itself, is simply the cultivation of the intellect, as such, and its object is nothing more or less than intellectual excel-

---

38   Paul Misner, 'The "liberal" legacy of John Henry Newman' in *Newman and the Modernists* (Lanham, Md: University Press of America, 1985), 5. According to Kenny, Newman 'sympathized warmly with the general policy and sentiment of Lacordaire, and Montalembert, and still more of Dupanloup'. See Terrence Kenny, *The Political Thought of John Henry Newman* (London: Longman, Green and Co., 1957), 151.

39   *The Idea of a University*,
     http://www.newmanreader. org/works/idea/discourse5.html, 114.

lence. Every thing has its own perfection, be it higher or lower in the scale of things; and the perfection of one is not the perfection of another'.[40]

In *The Idea of a University*, Newman also teaches that 'all knowledge forms one whole, because its subject-matter is one; for the universe in its length and breadth is so intimately knit together'.[41] He was influenced by the Church Fathers who in turn were influenced by Greek philosophers, including Plato and Aristotle, and his idea of liberal education lies in this spiritual vision of oneness. Newman stood for 'integration, philosophy, intuition and faith', at a time of increasing rationalism and secularism, and he defended the ideal of a liberal education as opposed to pragmatic and utilitarian training.[42] Even theology is not the exclusive property of one people or creed and this 'ancient, this far-spreading philosophy' can be found in various religions and Christian denominations. God is the sole source of everything that is good, true and beautiful, including pagan literature and religion.[43]

Newman had great admiration for pagan classics; he thought that Xenophon was one of the 'best principled and most religious' writers who ever lived and that the Roman poet Virgil was a prophet whose words were oracles that spoke directly to the human heart.[44] He believed that all true art, regardless of origins, is part of divine revelation, and the great orators of ancient Greece had articulated a 'beautiful idea' which could reach perfection in the coming of Christ's kingdom.[45] Newman's understanding of the role of conscience came from his study of the classics, and he thought that Greek ethics was too

40 Ibid., 121.
41 Ibid., 50.
42 David Walsh, 'Newman on the Secular Need for a Religious Education', *Faith and Reason* (1992), 359-360.
43 Francis McGrath, *John Henry Newman: Universal Revelation* (Mulgrave, Victoria: John Garratt Publishing, 1977), 86.
44 *Sermons Preached on Various Occasions*, http://www.newmanreader.org /works/occasions/ sermon2.html, 23.
45 Francis McGrath, *John Henry Newman: Universal Revelation* (Mulgrave, Victoria: John Garratt Publishing, 1977), 87.

close to Christian ethics to be coincidence.[46] The church and scripture are ordinary channels of revelation, but they are not the only ones. He believed all genuine religions rooted in nature or the supernatural are part of God's plan of salvation and divine truth comes to us through a variety of channels including Greek classics, philosophy and the sacred books of other religions.[47]

The establishment of public reading rooms in England in the nineteenth century was meant to promote a new spirit of universal utilitarian education. This was based on the conviction that education was best served by the cultivation of 'useful knowledge [as] the great instrument of education'.[48] It was believed that knowledge can make us better because human being 'by being accustomed to such contemplations will feel the moral dignity of his nature exalted'.[49] In 'The Tamworth Reading Room', Newman, however, argues that development in physical science is not going to improve our morals, and that without the influence of Christianity, the mere acquisition of knowledge will lead to pride in one's own achievement. Men are not moved by reason, and in the absence of spiritual education, 'the inevitable human tendency toward self-aggrandizement is given free rein'.[50]

Science also cannot lead people to recognise the seriousness of sin and the need for redemption, and the study of nature will not lead people to contemplate the creator. In the absence of religious feeling, Newman contends, the mind will be led to atheism as the simplest and easiest theory. Even when a person is spiritually disposed, he may not be able to discover the Christian God, but something like 'the animated principle of a vast and complicated system', 'world soul', 'vital power', or 'the Supreme Being', as what John Hick has advocated.

---

46   Ibid.
47   Ibid., 88.
48   *Discussions and Arguments*, 'The Tamworth Reading Room', http://www. newmanreader.org/works/ arguments/tamworth/section1.html, 255.
49   Ibid., http://www.newmanreader.org/works/arguments/tamworth/section2.html, 261.
50   David Walsh, 'Newman on the Secular Need for a Religious Education', *Faith and Reason* (1992), 363.

But for Newman, the essence of religion is 'the idea of a Moral Governor and a particular Providence', and we can comprehend this only through a realisation of sin and redemption in the Christian sense. [51] Thus, Newman believes the cultivation of this religious sense that should form the basis of education. He perceives the danger in the separation of education and disciplines from the spiritual life of man, which assures him of meaning, rationality and goodness of their knowledge. This critical dissociation occurs when the force of spiritual truth not only loses its power to command obedience, but is reduced to purely subjective emotion, where truth and falsity, right and wrong do not have significance.

Although Newman criticised liberalism for its anti-dogmatic principle, he was against dogmatism. In his Oxford University sermon on 'Wisdom as Contrasted with Faith and with Bigotry', dogmatism is characterised as bigotry, the application of narrow principles. He says that 'our presumptions ... deserve the name of bigotry and dogmatism [when] ... we make a wrong use of such light as given us, and mistake what is a lantern unto our feet for the sun in the heavens ... Bigotry professes to understand what it maintains, though it does not; ... it persists, not in abandoning argument, but in arguing only in one way'. [52]

This narrow-minded dogmatism or conservatism is the opposite of the enlargement of the mind which is the aim of liberal education, as Newman advocates in *The Idea of a University*: the cultivation, illumination, and opening of the mind that is no longer confined to an ego-centric view of the world. Newman writes:

> [The student] apprehends the great outlines of knowledge, the principles on which it rests, the scale of its parts, its lights and its shades, its great points and its little, as he otherwise cannot apprehend them. Hence it is that his education is called 'Liberal'. A habit of mind is formed which lasts through life, of which the attributes are, freedom, equitableness, calmness, moderation, and wisdom; or

---

51 Ibid., 364.
52 Quoted Mary Katherine Tillman, 'Newman: the dialectic of 'liberalism' and 'conservatism',' *Josephinum Journal of Theology* 9, no. 2 (Sum-Fall 2002), 189.

what in a former Discourse I have ventured to call a philosophical habit. This then I would assign as the special fruit of the education furnished at a University, as contrasted with other places of teaching or modes of teaching. This is the main purpose of a University in its treatment of its students.[53]

Biblical Criticism

Newman was aware of the Bible's ambiguities, indeterminacies, and openness to many interpretations, which may lead to misreading and heresy. He grappled with issues like that, which later led him to be labelled modernist. According to T. Wright, 'He [Newman] comes to us as a modern', the 'child of British empiricism ... overlaid with Romanticism', 'hypersensitive to epistemological issues, concerned with the psychology of impressions and ideas, agnostic about their object'.[54] Newman's scepticism about our obtaining objective knowledge of ultimate truth brings him 'remarkably close to what may be termed a "postmodern" perspective'.[55]

Newman's recognition of the Bible's openness to many differing interpretations is seen not as a weakness but 'as a product of its inner life and creativity, its openness to the operations of grace'.[56] He remained orthodox because he submitted wholeheartedly to the teaching

53   *The Idea of a University*,
      http://www.newmanreader.org/works/idea/discourse5.html, 101-102.
54   Quoted in T.R. Wright, 'Newman on the Bible: a *Via Media* to Postmodernity'
      in *Newman and the Word*, edited by Terrence Merrigan and Ian T. Ker (Louvain: Peeters Press, 2000), 218. Basil Mitchell claims that Newman was firmly rooted in the empiricist tradition of Locke and Hume. He was also influenced by the Romantic preoccupation with the interior life and historical process, but not Schleiermacher's understanding of Christian dogma as expression of emotion, imagination or will. See Basil Mitchell, 'Newman as a Philospher', in *Newman after a Hundred Years*, edited by Ian Ker and Alan G. Hill (Oxford: Clarendon Press, 1990), 223.
55   Ibid.
56   Ibid., 219.

authority of the church, even though Newman's belief fell well short of absolute truth. In post-modernity, John Milbank says, 'there are infinitely many possible versions of truth, inseparable from particular narratives'.[57] Thus, Wright argues that 'Newman can be said to anticipate post modernity in particular in his awareness of textuality, the limits of language, the phenomenologically peculiar status of written marks, seemingly objective on the page but only coming to life in the minds of their readers'.[58]

In his *University Sermons* Newman teaches that words are inadequate to express reality and even scripture is limited, and thus, 'God has condescended to speak to us so far as human thought and language will admit, by approximations'.[59] He saw precision in language as 'an act of Arian insolence', and his own language is so rich with metaphors, ambiguities and complexities, and at times, even confusing.[60] Newman accepts the fact that men continually misinterpret scripture, but believes that they usually misinterpret the accidents of faith and not the fundamentals. Schism occurs within the church when there are differences, and it is not that the Scriptures speaks variously, but that the church has failed to resolve the question of interpretation.[61]

Wright argues that Newman's understanding of the complexities of the reading process and the prejudices and prepossessions that people bring to the text is close to the post-modern pragmatic reader-response theory of Stanley Fish. Newman believes most people cannot contemplate scripture without bringing in their own interpretation

57   Ibid.
58   T.R. Wright, 'Newman on the Bible: a *Via Media* to Postmodernity' in *Newman and the Word*, edited by Terrence Merrigan and Ian T. Ker (Louvain: Peeters Press, 2000), 220.
59   *Oxford University Sermons*,
      http://www.newmanreader.org/works/oxford/sermon13.html, 269.
60   Quoted in T.R. Wright, 'Newman on the Bible: a *Via Media* to Postmodernity' in *Newman and the Word*, edited by Terrence Merrigan and Ian T. Ker (Louvain: Peeters Press, 2000), 222.
61   T.R. Wright, 'Newman on the Bible: a *Via Media* to Postmodernity' in *Newman and the Word*, edited by Terrence Merrigan and Ian T. Ker (Louvain: Peeters Press, 2000), 226.

which they inherit from their education, and different people have different abilities in reading the scripture.[62]

In the area of biblical criticism, Newman also encouraged free discussion and was against premature closure of open questions. The aim of his 1884 articles on biblical inspiration was to establish that theologians had no *a priori* right to settle open questions on inspiration and inerrancy without examining them in new contexts. He published his essay 'On the Inspiration of Scripture' in February 1884, which alluded to the difficulties of pseudonymous attributions of biblical books to a Moses or a David; the several authors of a book such as Genesis or Isaiah; the assimilation of pagan sources or traditions and the incorporation of profane writings.[63] Newman was aware that the question of inspiration could raise problem for educated modern believers or would-be believers.

Theology of the Laity

Newman lived at a time when the church was highly clerical, the laity had only a passive role, and theological debate was limited. Miller says Newman's vision of the church was 'pastoral' in the sense that he wanted more involvement of the laity in church affairs, to reclaim what was initially their rightful role.[64] Newman rightly said to his bishop that the church would look foolish without the laity, because they were an active force in the church and society. His experience at Oxford convinced him that an educated Catholic laity would form the public mind and exert moral influence on the world. In this, Newman was a liberal and at odds with the prevailing 'hierarchology' – Roman

62   Ibid., 227.
63   Paul Misner, 'The "liberal" legacy of John Henry Newman' in *Newman and the Modernists* (Lanham, Md: University Press of America, 1985), 18.
64   Edward Jeremy Miller, *John Henry Newman on the Idea of Church* (West Virginia: The Patmos Press, 1987), 59.

machinery bend on controlling the faithful.[65] He believed that lay people should work hand in hand with church authorities to discern the will of God, and the Christian message is realized in the fellowship of hierarchy and laity which constitutes what Vatican II calls 'the people of God'.[66]

The laity's personal experience of Christian life is not a replica of clerical life – they live in the secular world, and thus their experience is unique and a source of distinctive insight which they can bring to the ministry. Newman believed the laity can offer unique perspective into revelation because of their involvement in the world. His stress was on the entire people of God at the service of the Gospel message, and he also advocated a type of evangelization based on personal influence: 'The great instrument of propagating moral truth is personal knowledge'.[67] Newman was right to stress that people are more influenced by the personal examples than by someone's ability to discuss Christian apologetics.

To be effective in evangelisation, the laity must be grounded in revealed doctrines, competent in the intellectual disciplines and affairs of the world. Thus, Newman was convinced that the church must support higher education for its laity, although he was quick to add that this kind of superior education cannot be a translated version of seminary training for the priests. He was attempting to establish a Catholic university in Dublin based on the Oxford model. The other alternative was to establish a Catholic college at Oxford or Cambridge, or have Catholic youth attending one of the existing colleges. Unfortunately, Newman failed in his educational endeavours: in his opinion, the bishop resisted having a Catholic university which they could not control. The Vatican also prohibited starting a Catholic college at Oxford, and discouraged parents from sending their children to existing col-

65   Ibid., 63.
66   *Lumen Gentium*,
     http://www.vatican.va/archive/hist_councils/ii_ vatican_council/documents/vat-
     ii_const_19641121_lumen-gentium_en.html, chapter 2.
67   *Lectures on the Present Position of Catholics in England,* http://www. newman-
     reader.org/ works/england/ lecture9.html, 381.

leges because they thought it would endanger their faith. The real reason, Newman rightly believed was the clergy's fear of losing control because an educated and articulated laity would no longer be docile. An independent-minded and competent laity was worse than the threat of secularism, the church believed.[68]

The church was afraid an educated laity would be unmanageable, but Newman feared that poorly educated laity would turn anti-clerical without confidence in church leadership. He was convinced that an educated laity would be the strength of the church if they were to be given trust and responsibility instead of authoritarian control which stifled their creativity and energy. It was painful for Newman to see the talents of convert Anglicans wasted because the church feared an educated and initiative-taking laity: 'It has always been a real grief, and almost wound which I have carried with me, that married and especially clerically married converts, have been so tossed aside, and suffered to live or die as they may. We have lost a vast deal of power and zeal, of high talents and devotion, which might have done much for the glory of God'.[69]

Hence, Newman's theology of the laity is based on the unique experience of men and women working in the secular world which they can bring to the church to help in evangelisation. The Christian message will be reflected in their discernments which cannot be found in the experience of the hierarchy. If the church were to be bent on controlling the minds of the laity by denying them higher education, the church would be impoverished. Newman rightly attributed the fear of an educated and involved laity to the Latin mentality's need for control and uniformity. He could foresee that the Latin race would no longer have charge of the Magisterium in the church, and he counselled patience for God works in his own time.[70]

---

68   Edward Jeremy Miller, *John Henry Newman on the Idea of Church* (West Virginia: The Patmos Press, 1987), 67.
69   Quoted in Edward Jeremy Miller, *John Henry Newman on the Idea of Church* (West Virginia: The Patmos Press, 1987), 68.
70   Ibid., 68-69.

Sensus Fidelium

In his studies of church history, Newman found that the function of transmitting and formulating the faith had not always been carried out properly by the ecclesiastical authorities. In *Arians of the Fourth Century*, Newman teaches that it is the *sensus fidelium* (sense of the faithful) of the people and not the Magisterium or teaching authority of the bishops that maintained the Catholic faith in the aftermath of the Arian controversy:

> The episcopate, whose action was so prompt and concordant at Nicea on the rise of Arianism, did not, as a class or order of men, play a good part in the troubles consequent upon the Council; and the laity did. The Catholic people, in the length and breadth of Christendom, were the obstinate champions of Catholic truth, and the bishops were not.[71]

He avoided the simplistic distinction between clerics and non-clerical teachers by extending the term 'faithful' to everyone in the church:

> In speaking of the laity, I speak inclusively of their parish-priests (so to call them), at least in many places; but on the whole, taking a wide view of the history, we are obliged to say that the governing body of the Church came short, and the governed were pre-eminent in faith, zeal, courage, and constancy.[72]

The Magisterium of the church in Newman's time as well as in our own is one sure note of catholic unity and it 'is situated here *within* the living instinct for faith possessed by all the faithful, and not apart from it or even formally prior to it'.[73] In each part of the church, everyone

---

71   *Arians of the Fourth Century*,
     http://www.newmanreader.org/works/arians/note5.html, 445.
72   Ibid.
73   Paul G. Crowley, S.J., 'The *Sensus Fidelium* and Catholicity: Newman's Legacy in the Age of the Inculturation', in *John Henry Newman: Theology and Reform*, edited by Michael E. Allsopp and Ronald R. Burke (New York: Garland Publishing, Inc., 1992), 115.

has a distinct role to play. But in the Arian controversy, Newman demonstrates his principle that the *sensus fidelium* is the guardian of the Catholic faith in times of uncertainty in the church. His treatment of this ancient controversy is novel because he treats it not as a doctrinal problem but as an ecclesial problem. Newman pits 'different senses of faith against one another in a struggle over the meaning and practice of faith'.[74]

According to Paul Crowley, the Arian controversy reflects how the faithful maintained orthodoxy in a cultural situation that was different from that of mainstream churches in the empire. It is an example of the conflict between the Catholic faith and its 'inculturated theological forms'. The faithful experienced the tension and held fast to their understanding of the Catholic faith, 'though with distinctive local flourishes, ranging from riots to *anachoresis*'.[75] For Newman, the Arian controversy was not just about ideas abstracted from history. It involved the creed which became the battleground of the bishops in their struggle over authority. It also concerned all the people in the church of Egypt and beyond, because it involved the local expressions of faith.[76] Viewed in this light, Newman's appeal to the *sensus fidelium* as the mainstay of the Catholic faith during the Arian controversy is a profound theological principle, and this is still relevant today as we see the rise of new theologies from the third world challenging the traditional western theological discourse.

Newman's treatment of *sensus fidelium* pertains to the reception and transmission of the faith in its doctrinal forms. His most enduring contribution, which led many to regard him as a liberal is the claim he made that the faith is transmitted and received by the faithful themselves, by the entire church of a particular time and place, in a special relationship with the church authority. It is in the faith of the people, Newman claims, that the catholicity of the faith is safeguarded. This claim continues to challenge us because the church cannot escape the

74   Ibid.,116. See also *Arians of the Fourth Century*, Appendix Note V, http://www. newmanreader.org/ works/arians/note5.html, 445-468.
75   Ibid., 117.
76   Ibid.

tension between a universal teaching function and the various theologies that spring up from diverse cultural situations. In Newman's perception, it is the people who are taught, in a particular place, who become the universal teacher. The present situation of religious pluralism in Asia means that local Christian churches in their encounter with the great spiritual traditions of Asia, constitutes a new situation, which requires new answers.

In view of this, we can look to Newman's teaching to resolve the tension between catholicity and inculturation in our day, and to draw out its implications. According to Crowley, a good example of this is the theology of liberation:

> The theology of liberation rests upon an assertion of a church model that begins with the *sensus fidelium*, not with hierarchical structures. It challenges other theological streams within the church, including those expressed by the hierarchical magisterium, to listen and to become engaged with the legitimate mediations of the faith tradition that have taken place within the local church contexts.[77]

Newman would never have imagined that his ideas could be used to resolve the tensions between official church teaching and a local theology that springs out of a specific economic-political situation; the situation in Latin America is far from the idyllic world of Victorian England. But the idea of *sensus fidelium*, inspired by Newman, could serve as a tool in resolving the tension between the catholicity of faith and its cultural manifestation of the catholicity. His use of the *sensus fidelium* comes from the principle taken from his work on the development of Christian doctrines. This work looks upon Christian truth as undergoing development which is grasped vaguely but becomes clear through time or under the catalyst of some challenges. The official vision of the church is institutional and hierarchical, but Newman's idea of the church is organic and communal. That Crowley is able to associate Newman's *sensus fidelium* with the theology of liberation is a testimony of his liberal spirit and legacy.

---

77 Ibid., 123.

Newman rightly felt that a conservative and over-centralised church might lose the laity if the latter have no involvement in the process by which revelation is discerned: they are reduced to having an 'implicit faith'. The educated class will end up in indifference, and the poor class in superstition. If doctrines are imposed from the top without taking into consideration people's experience and insight, then the laity are likely to become alienated by the church and by the message intended by God to strengthen their faith. Newman realised that the ecclesiastical authorities cannot afford to prevent the laity from the process of discernment. Miller rightly argues that Newman was farsighted to perceive that the challenge to ministry would come from secular life: 'The philosophy of the day, its literature, and especially the growing techno-scientific ethos had abandoned Christian roots and were distinct to clash with religion. Educated, committed laity were the proper witnesses to a living faith and were the best evangelisers of the secularist society that was surely coming'.[78]

Consulting the Faithful in Matters of Doctrine

'What is the province of the laity? To hunt, to shoot, to entertain', wrote Monsignor George Talbot in response to Newman's 'On Consulting the Faithful in Matters of Doctrine', which was published in the *Rambler* in July, 1859. John Coulson says Newman's publication of this essay 'was an act of political suicide from which his career within the church was never fully to recover; at one stroke he, whose reputation is the one honest broker between the extremes of English Catholic opinion had hitherto stood untarnished, gained the Pope's personal displeasure, the reputation at Rome of being the most dangerous man in England, and a formal accusation of heresy proffered

---

78   Edward Jeremy Miller, *John Henry Newman on the Idea of Church* (West Virginia: The Patmos Press, 1987), 75.

against him by the Bishop of Newport'. Talbot believed that the laity are in the church to 'pray up, pay up and shut up!'[79]

Although the hierarchy is responsible for defining and enforcing the church tradition, Newman insists the laity must be consulted because 'The body of the faithful is one of the witnesses to the fact of the tradition of revealed doctrine... their consensus through Christendom is the voice of the Infallible Church'.[80] At the same time he also states that the power and prerogative of defining dogmas rest exclusively with Magisterium.[81] To 'consult' means to seek an opinion, but it can also mean to find out something as when one consults a barometer. According to Newman, consulting the 'sense of the faithful' means ascertaining in fact what the laity believes. This actually took place when the bishops consulted the faithful six years before the promulgation of the Immaculate Conception in 1854. Newman also located infallibility in the totality of the church, which means the laity as well as the hierarchy: 'Infallibility resides in the laity and Magisterium in a unitary way, as a figure is contained both on the seal (Magisterium) and on the wax (laity)'.[82]

Newman observes, as we have seen earlier in the Arian controversy, that although in the fourth century there were bishops and saints like Athanasius and Ambrose, 'nevertheless in that very day the divine tradition committed to the infallible Church was proclaimed and maintained far more by the faithful than by the Episcopate'.[83] The laity in

79   See Michael Sharkey, 'Newman on the Laity',
      http://www.ewtn.com/library/Theology/NEWMNLAY.HTM.
80   'On   Consulting   the   Faithful   in   Matters   of   Doctrine',
      http://www.newmanreader.org/works/ rambler/consulting.html, 205.
81   Mary Katherine Tillman, 'Newman: the dialectic of 'liberalism' and 'conservatism',' *Josephinum Journal of Theology* 9, no. 2 (Sum-Fall 2002), 183.
82   Edward Jeremy Miller, *John Henry Newman on the Idea of Church* (West Virginia: The Patmos Press, 1987), 71.
83   'On Consulting the Faithful in Matters of Doctrine',
      http://www.newmanreader. org/works/ rambler/consulting.html, 213. Gunton sees this work as a sincere desire of Newman to develop a communal rather than a merely clerical conception of the nature of authority. As a result of this writing, Newman became a suspect in high places. See Colin Gunton, 'Newman's

Newman's understanding is not merely a stamp, and he maintains the possibility of bishops teaching heretical doctrines while the laity hold fast to orthodoxy.

During the Arian heresy, 'in that time of immense confusion the divine dogma of our Lord's divinity was proclaimed, enforced, maintained, and (humanly speaking) preserved, far more by the 'Ecclesia docta' than by the 'Ecclesia docens' ... the body of the episcopate was unfaithful to its commission, while the body of the laity was faithful to its baptism'.[84] He concludes by saying that 'there was a temporary suspense of the functions' of the teaching church, the unpalatable truth being that the 'body of Bishops failed in their confession of the faith'.[85]

The danger now, he asserts, is that when the hierarchy is sound and faithful, the laity would be neglected and relegated to being an audience or, at best, playing a supporting role. This kind of liberal understanding of the role of laity in the church did not go over well with church authorities, and Newman remained under a cloud of Vatican suspicion for years.

'On Consulting the Faithful in Matters of Doctrine', is actually a tract against the bishops because the faithful includes priests and religious. According to Ian Ker, the origin of the essay lay in Newman's concern about the English bishops who did not hold consultations with the laity regarding the Royal Commission and the state of primary education. At a deeper theological level, Newman taught that faith did not belong to the bishops alone, but to the whole people of God.[86] This was dramatically highlighted during the Arian heresy when the leadership failed to proclaim and teach the faith. And since faith is not the

---

Dialectic Dogma and Reason in the Seventy-Third *Tract for the Times*' in *Newman after a Hundred Years*, edited by Ian Ker and Alan G. Hill (Oxford: Clarendon Press, 1990), 312.

84   Ibid.

85   Ibid., 214.

86   Ian Ker, 'Newman on the *Consensus Fidelium* as "The Voice of The Infallible Church"', in *Newman and the Word*, edited by Terrence Merrigan and Ian T. Ker (Louvain: Peeters Press, 2000), 77.

property of the bishops alone, it was the body of laity that saved the faith. Newman lived in a highly clericalised church where the division of clergy and laity was sharp; he wanted to protect the rights of the laity or the whole body of the faithful.

Resisting the Spirit of Liberalism of his time

As mentioned before, Newman insisted the church must learn to cope with liberalism. This mindset of liberalism, according to him is characterised by scepticism, an inevitable consequence of the development of human reason. Liberalism is a way of thinking that operates without reference to the principles and doctrines of traditional religion; it originates in the empirical order or reason exercised by the natural man. Liberalism is pragmatism - it makes its presence felt first in the social and political arenas. Newman resisted liberalism only when it interfered with the rights and authority of the Established Church. In the fields of education, politics and even in church organisation, his outlook was liberal in many ways.

The Oxford Movement, as we have seen, was founded to resist liberalism and to restore the Anglican Church to its Catholic character. Newman explains in his *Apologia* that his involvement in the Movement was founded on the theological principle that the church has been given a revelation and her duty is to preserve, protect and defend it. It was felt the church was threatened by secularism. By the time he left the Anglican Church, Newman was convinced it did not have the resources to resist the onslaught of liberalism. Later he would accept the fact that liberalism was here to stay and would try to make the best of the situation. But in the beginning, Newman was championing a cause and not just the prevention of changes. He was fighting on behalf of revealed religion, and Merrigan has correctly argued that he was resisting the spirit of liberalism and not liberalism as such.[87] It is significant that Newman was fighting the spirit of liberalism of that particular time - the onslaught of secularism and the decline of Christianity.

J. M. Cameron warns us that it would be a mistake to see Newman merely as a young man who avoided the danger of liberalism of Whately in his early years at Oxford and remained the same in his attitude towards liberalism. In Rome, he had had the reputation of a strong liberal ever since he published his *Essay on the Development of Christian Doctrine* and 'On Consulting the Faithful in Matters of Doctrine'. Newman, in the note he added to the second edition of the *Apologia*, stated that we must go beyond calling liberalism the 'Anti-Dogmatic Principle' not just because this does not say much, but also there were great Catholic liberals like Montalembert and Lacordaire for whom Newman had great sympathies.[88]

Hastings comes up with a definition of liberalism applicable to both the secular and religious spheres: liberalism is a commitment to freedom in a society fragmented by the influence of rational enquiry, political efficiency and pluralism. It is opposed to the conservative commitment to control society on the basis of authority, including religious authority. Liberalism is a practical acceptance of social and intellectual pluralism. It seeks to get rid of the public authority of religion. It does not renounce the concept of truth, but renounces the right to impose truth on others. Acceptance of truth, according to the liberal, must be based on conviction or reason. It recognises that the formulation of truth is historically conditioned. The liberal stands for freedom, the anti-liberal is for public order; the liberal appeals to reason, while the anti-liberal appeals to authority, tradition, and revelation. The liberal is influenced by evolution and a sense of history.[89]

---

87   Terrence Merrigan, 'Newman and theological liberalism', *Theological Studies* 66, no. 3 (September 2005), 609.

88   J.M. Cameron, 'Newman and Liberalism', *Cross Currents* 30, no. 2 (Summer 1980), 155.

89   Adrian Hastings, *The Theology of a Protestant Catholic* (Philadelphia: Trinity Press International, 1990), 119.

Based on Hastings' definition of liberalism, we can see how closely Newman identified with some of the features of liberal thought, and at the same time he stood for authority, tradition and revelation. Newman's liberal spirit is relevant to inter-faith dialogue and understanding of Christianity in relation to other religions. Although he was a devout Christian, Newman believed humanity always has 'the guidance of Tradition, in addition to those internal notions of right and wrong which the Spirit has put into the heart of each individual'.[90] In view of this, the following chapter attempts to explore Newman's theology of religions.

---

90   *Arians of the Fourth Century,*
       http://www.newmanreader.org /works/arians/chapter1–3.html, 80.

Chapter 5

Newman's Liberalism in the Context of Contemporary Pluralism

In the last two chapters, I have sought to cast light on Newman's understanding of liberalism, engaging in various primary and secondary sources to find out which aspects of his ideas are liberal and which are not. As we have seen, the word 'liberalism' carries heavy historical baggage and depends on how it is understood and in what context.

Trailing his liberal spirit, seeing him as a theologically progressive genius, this chapter is a culmination of Newman's liberal ideas – his understanding of non-Christian religions in relation to Christianity. One of his first principles is his insistence on the historical nature of God's revelation and continuing self-communication. The application of this first principle of his liberal thought can help us to access the claims of the pluralist, inclusivist, and exclusivist theology of religions.

The Vatican document, *Dominus Iesus* (2000), deals with the challenges posed to Christianity, the rise of religious pluralism, and seeks to defend the unity of the economy of salvation and the incarnational principle in the Christian faith. It insists on the trinitarian character of God and the necessity of the invisible church which continues Christ's saving work. These claims have been challenged by the pluralist theology of religions that views Christian faith like every other religious tradition, which can be interpreted in one perspective, one world view, and which has developed alongside with other religions in history. Gordon D. Kaufman argues that 'when one applies the concept 'world view' to one's own tradition in this way, one simultaneously distinguishes it from and relates it to other world views'. The knowledge of fundamental categories found in Christianity can be applied to understanding other religions.[1] In the writings of Newman, there are also categories that he uses in relation to Christianity and natural religion.

The issue of religious pluralism is important because Christians find it increasingly difficult to claim an exclusivist or absolutist position regarding their faith today. There are some Christian theologians who even advance the idea that other religious communities and traditions can lead humankind towards transcendence or 'the ultimate reality', providing them the resources to interpret and orientate their human existence. It would be self-impoverishment if Christians refuse to learn from other religious traditions simply because there are other ways of being human. On the other hand, we can also question how much pluralism we can tolerate, especially with people who oppose our idea of liberty and way of life.[2]

Christianity was the first of the world's religious traditions to be deeply affected by the onslaught of new scientific and empirical knowledge and the secularization of society – it was the first major faith in the world to be transformed by modernity. The progress of secularization challenges Christians 'to develop forms of faith through which the human spirit can be transformingly related to the Transcendent within the context of our modern knowledge of ourselves and of our environment'.[3] Newman was aware of this modernizing trend and had stood up to the challenge in ways that were prophetic and original.

However, Newman was the product of the nineteenth century and we must place him in that context. Ignorant of Asian religious traditions and cultures, and lacking in historical consciousness, he spoke of

---

1   Gordon D. Kaufman, 'Religious Diversity, Historical Consciousness, and Christian Theology', in *The Myth of Christian Uniqueness*, edited by John Hick and Paul F. Knitter (London: SCM Press Ltd., 1987), 9.

2   See Erik Sidenvall, *After Anti–Catholicism?* (London: T&T Clark International, 2005), 1–7.

3   John Hick, 'The Non–Absoluteness of Christianity', in *The Myth of Christian Uniqueness*, edited by John Hick, and Paul F. Knitter (London: SCM Press Ltd., 1987), 26.

China as 'a huge, stationary, unattractive, morose civilization'.[4] This is not at all surprising for a Victorian gentleman like Newman, and at that time, the attitude of Christian churches towards other religious communities was distorted and ill–informed. Wilfred Cantwell Smith believes this wrong attitude grew out of compassion and noble concern as it was 'a virtue misguided by misunderstanding, distorted by misapprehension'.[5] Newman certainly falls under this category. Although he was ignorant of oriental religious traditions, Newman was well acquainted with the Classics, Greek and Roman religions, and was certainly aware that religious spirit and practice are present outside Christianity. Nonetheless, his analysis of religion is based on moral grounds:

> I take our natural perception of right and wrong as the standard for determining the characteristics of Natural Religion, and I use the religious rites and traditions which are actually found in the world, only so far as they agree with our moral sense ... no religion is from God which contradicts our sense of right and wrong.[6]

According to Merrigan, Newman's continuing relevance is sought not in his discussions of particular topics which are contextual, but in 'first principles' and his greatest contribution to the theology of religions is his insistence on the historical character of God's self-revelation.[7]

We live in an interdependent, interconnected globalised village, and it is no longer possible to ignore other ways of becoming and believing. Christians need to meet people of other religious traditions on

---

4   *The Idea of a University,*
    http://www.newmanreader.org/works/idea/article1.html, 252.
5   Wilfred Cantwell Smith, 'Idolatry', in *The Myth of Christian Uniqueness*, edited by John Hick and Paul F. Knitter (London: SCM Press Ltd., 1987), 54.
6   *An Essay in Aid of a Grammar of Assent,*
    http://www.newmanreader.org/works/grammar/ chapter10–2.html,419.
7   Terrence Merrigan, 'Christianity and the Non–Christian Religions in the Light of the Theology of John Henry Newman', *Irish Theological Quarterly* 68 (2003), 345.

an equal footing, seek to understand and appreciate their unique insights into the human condition, their beliefs and practices, some of which are older than Christianity itself. None of us, Christians or non-Christians, has the absolute truth and answer to deal with the enormous problems that life presents. In this respect Newman can provide us with a balanced approach towards appreciating other religious traditions while standing firm on our conviction about the truth of Christianity.

Besides his own faith in Christianity, Newman was aware that tradition and the role of conscience can lead people towards the truth. His attitude towards paganism reveals a remarkable liberality although he condemned heresy. Although he was generally opposed to the idea of inevitable change and progress, Newman was in many ways a beneficiary of this growing liberal atmosphere.

However, conscious of his relationship to God, Newman always remained grounded in his deep understanding of the majestic presence of God. Having lived through almost the whole of the nineteenth century (1801-1890), he had witnessed firsthand many intellectual conflicts of that time, conflicts that are still raging today. He strode two worlds at once: a traditional Christian world and a modern secular one. Owen Chadwick argues that 'he was the first theorist of Christian doctrine to face the challenge of modern historical enquiry'.[8]

Pluralist Theology of Religion

The pluralist school of theologians represented by John Hick, Paul Knitter and Wilfred Cantwell Smith are opposed to Christianity's claim of superiority, universality and definitiveness. At the same time they affirm the independent validity of other means to salvation. The pluralists reject *exclusivism* which believes Christianity is the only

8   Owen Chadwick, *Newman* (Oxford: Oxford University Press, 1983), 3.

way to salvation. It attempts to go beyond *inclusivism* which acknowledges the positive role played by other religious traditions, but considers Christ as the normative symbol of salvation, and the Christian faith as the completion of every religious system.[9]

Merrigan believes the pluralist paradigm suits the post-modern age because it stresses present religious experience and is opposed to historical revelation.[10] Religious pluralists also insist on the ultimate mysterious nature of the divine reality, and believe we cannot adequately grasp God because of the fact that there are many religious traditions in the world. They downplay the difference between religions and describe them as complementary or historically conditioned.

A pluralist like Hick appeals to the Kantian distinction between the 'noumenal world', which exists independently of man's perception of it, and the 'phenomenal world', which is the world as it appears to him.[11] He classifies this 'noumenal world' as 'the Real *an sich'* (in itself) which is not an object of cult and cannot be experienced directly, and thus it can only appear in terms of various human forms. It is the ultimate reality which transcends reality and cannot be known, and as such, the object of our faith is just a human construct.[12]

Hick's vision of a pluralistic Christianity implies we can only worship God and not Jesus, because he is just a mediator. Naturally, Newman's understanding of religion as a rite, creed, philosophy and duty is far removed from the pluralistic view. However, Merrigan argues that his defence of lived religion provides lessons for the pluralists as well as for the inclusivists.[13]

9   John Hick and Paul F. Knitter, 'Introduction', in *The Myth of Christian Uniqueness,* edited by John Hick and Paul Knitter (London: SCM Press: 1987), viii.

10   Terrence Merrigan, 'The Anthropology of Conversion: Newman and the Contemporary Theology of Religions', in *Newman and Conversion*, edited by Ian Ker (Edinburgh: T& T Clarke, 1997), 120.

11   Gavin D'Costa, *John Hick's Theology of Religions* (Lanham: University Press of America), 157.

12   John Hick, *The Metaphor of God Incarnate* (London: SCM, 1993), 140–141.

13   Terrence Merrigan, 'Christianity and the Non–Christian Religions in the Light of the Theology of John Henry Newman', *Irish Theological Quarterly* 68 (2003), 351.

Inclusivist Theology of Religions

Religious inclusivists believe Christ is always implicated in the saving action of God and regard the Christian faith as the fulfilment of other religions. This approach has been adopted by the Second Vatican Council in its document on non-Christian religions, *Nostra Aetate* (1965), which signalled a new attitude on the part of the Roman Catholic Church towards other faiths and a willingness to recognise their positive contribution to humanity. Great non-Christian religions are seen as expressions of genuine human longing to answer the most fundamental question regarding our human existence.

The Council teaches that salvific grace can operate in the hearts of those outside the church, even in those who do not believe in God.[14] Inclusivist theologians like Karl Rahner, Hans Küng and Jacques Dupuis have adopted this new appreciation of non-Christian religions into a comprehensive Christian theology of religions and seek to portray Christ as the source of saving grace in all religions.

The Document *Dialogue and Proclamation* issued in 1991 by the Pontifical Council for Interreligious Dialogue and the Congregation for the Evangelization of Peoples acknowledges that 'concretely, it will be in the sincere practice of what is good in their own religious traditions and by following the dictates of their conscience that the members of other religions respond positively to God's invitation and receive salvation in Jesus Christ, even while they do not recognize or acknowledge him as their saviour'.[15]

---

14 *Nostra Aetate,* Declaration on the Relation of the Church to Non–Christian Religions (1965),
http://www.vatican.va/archive/hist_councils/ii_vatican_council/documents/vat–ii_decl_19651028_nostra–aetate_en.html, 1–2.

15 *Dialogue and Proclamation*, Pontifical Council for Inter–Religious Dialogue, http://www.vatican.va/ roman_curia/pontifical_councils/interelg/documents/rc_pc_interelg_doc_19051991 dialogue–and–proclamatio_en.html, 29.

Exclusivist Theology of Religions

Gavin D'Costa in his *Christianity and World Religions* fine tunes his understanding of the different Christian theological responses to world religions. I would like to focus this discussion on the positions of restrictivist inclusivists, restrictive–access exclusivists (RAE) and universal access exclusivists (UAE) as they relate to Newman's theology of religions. Like D'Costa, Newman was no pluralist and he would gladly endorse the view of Vatican II that Jesus is the definitive and normative means to salvation, and he would oppose the post-modern idea that all traditions are relative and Christianity does not have universal significance. Terrence Merrigan, however, argues that Newman's portrayal of 'natural religion' is close to post-modern sensibility and can serve as a guide to the pluralist and inclusivist views of the theology of religions.[16] Hence, Newman was traditional in one way and liberal in another, towards non-Christian religions.

Restrictivist inclusivists uphold the specific nature of Christian nature with Christ as the norm and baptism as the means to salvation. They acknowledge that not everyone has the opportunity to hear the Gospel, and so God makes provision through various means: natural law inscribed in the universe; in the heart through conscience; or the true and good elements in non-Christian religions. Other religions are not accepted *per se* as means of salvation, but act at best as preparation (*preparatio*) for the Gospel, and 'Christ is ontologically and causally exclusive to salvation, not epistemologically'.[17]

D'Costa supports what he calls universal-access exclusivism in the following rules. The first is that not everybody has the chance to hear the Gospel, but *fides ex auditu* (faith comes from hearing) requires that all must have this opportunity to attain salvation. Thus, the

---

16 Terrence Merrigan, 'The Anthropology of Conversion: Newman and the Contemporary Theology of Religions', in *Newman and Conversion*, edited by Ian Ker (Edinburgh: T& T Clarke, 1997), 119.
17 Gavin D'Costa, *Christianity and World Religions* (Oxford: Wiley–Blackwell, 2009), 24.

Catholic Ladislaus Boros believes there will be a chance to respond to the Gospel at the point of death; for the Protestant George Lindbeck, it is after death in a post-mortem state; and for the Catholic Joseph A. DiNoia, it is in purgatory. The second rule is that explicit faith and baptism are the normal ways to attain salvation, but there are other means that can serve as preparation to salvation. This can happen through revelation in nature, in following our conscience and reason, or through 'elements within a religion, but not through that religion *per se*'.[18]

This universal-access exclusivism is almost identical to the re-strictivist inclusivism position except for the qualification of a *preparatio* status and another qualification that requires the saved one to have specific knowledge of the Gospel and to participate in the life of the Trinity. D'Costa asserts that universal-access exclusivism affirms the positive elements in non-Christian religion and is the official Catholic position.[19]

In line with his support for this approach, he proposes a Roman Catholic trinitarian orientation towards other religions.[20] Although the teachings of Vatican II state that non-Christians may be saved, the church has not as yet recognised that there are 'salvific structures' in other faiths. The document *Nostra Aetate* is silent on this issue, and D'Costa thinks that this silence can be read in two differing ways. Depending on their understanding of grace and nature, some believe that non-Christian religions can be means of supernatural revelation. *Lumen Gentium* teaches that salvation may be obtained by those who 'sincerely seek God, and moved by His grace, strive by their deeds to do His will as it is known to them'.[21] In *Ad Gentes*, the church teaches that 'whatever good is found to be sown in the hearts and minds of

---

18   Ibid., 29.
19   Ibid.
20   Gavin D'Costa, *The Meeting of Religions and the Trinity* (New York: Orbis Books, Maryknoll, 2000), 99–142.
21   *Lumen Gentium,* Dogmatic Constitution on the Church (1964), http://www.vatican.va/archive/hist_councils/ii_vatican_council/documents/vat–iiconst 19641121lumen–gentiumen.html, 16.

men, or in the rites and cultures peculiar to various peoples, is not lost'.[22] D'Costa tries to show that the church does not give any straight forward answer as to whether non-Christian religions have salvific structures. He believes that this reservation or silence is intentional so as not to give any unqualified affirmation to other religions.[23]

In *Crossing the Threshold of Hope*, John Paul II acknowledges that elements in other religions may be used by the Holy Spirit in mediating grace: 'the Holy Spirit works effectively even outside the visible structure of the church, making use of these very *semina verbi*, that constitutes a kind of common soteriological root present in all religions'.[24] D'Costa cautions us in reading this statement as endorsing other religions as possible means of salvation. There is never a wholehearted 'yes' or 'no' – each historical case must be judged *a posteriori*. However, the main emphasis is the search for God as the core of all religions, and that God also works through our conscience and natural law.[25]

John Paul II sees the quest for God as the work of the Holy Spirit which is 'at the source of man's existential and religious questioning ...'.[26] In D'Costa's view, the stress on history is vital because grace works within a historical context. But the grace that operates in other religions is not the fullness of sanctifying and redeeming grace found only in Christ's Church. D'Costa asserts that 'all these actions of the Spirit cannot facilitate a theology of religions which affirms the various religious quests as authentic in themselves, apart from Christ, the

22 *Ad Gentes*, Decree on the Mission Activity of the Church (1965), http://www.vatican.va/archive/hist_councils/ii_vatican_council/ documents/vat–ii_decree_19651207_ad–gentes_en.html, 9.

23 Gavin D'Costa, *The Meeting of Religions and the Trinity* (New York: Orbis Books, Maryknoll, 2000), 105.

24 Ibid., 106.

25 Ibid.

26 John Paul II, *Redemptoris missio* (1990), http://www.vatican.va /holy_father/john_paul_ii/encyclicals/documents/hf_jp–iienc07121990redemptoris–missioen.html, 29.

Trinity, and the Church'.[27] D'Costa asserts that John Paul II maintains a fulfilment theory in that he acknowledges much that is true and holy in non-Christian religions. But the grace encountered in them is only a *preparatio evangelica*. It is only in the Church of Christ that grace is ordered towards eschatological fulfilment.[28]

Examining various church documents, D' Costa reaches the following conclusions: First, the church's silence or refusal to acknowledge other religions *per se* as salvific structures shows that pluralism or inclusivism are inappropriate ways to view other faiths. Second, it does not fail to acknowledge what is good and holy in other traditions, and Christians have much to learn from them. Third, non-Christians can be saved given various qualifications. Finally, the history of religions provides an important site for the working of God's spirit, and a theology of religions can be developed from this.[29]

Lumen Gentium asserts that the church is 'necessary for salvation'[30] and that whenever God is present, it is this triune God who is the foundation of the church. D'Costa goes one step further by saying the presence of the Holy Spirit in other religions is both trinitarian and ecclesiological. *Gaudium et Spes* maintains that the presence of the Spirit in other religions signifies 'a preparation for the Gospel'.[31] The document also acknowledges that elements of truth and goodness in western modernity may also be a preparation for the Gospel.[32] These

27 Gavin D'Costa, *The Meeting of Religions and the Trinity* (New York: Orbis Books, Maryknoll, 2000), 107.
28 Ibid., 109.
29 Ibid.
30 *Lumen Gentium,* Dogmatic Constitution on the Church (1964), http://www.vatican.va/archive/ hist_councils/ii_vatican_council/documents/vat–ii_const_19641121_lumen–gentium_en.html, 14.
31 *Gaudium et Spes*, Pastoral Constitution of the Church in the Modern Word (1965), http://www.vatican.va/archive/hist_councils/ii_vatican_council/ documents/vat–ii_cons_19651207_gaudium–et–spes_en.html#top, 29.
32 Ibid, 44.

elements may even challenge and change the church's formulation of doctrines and practices.[33]

D' Costa also points out that in *Redemptoris Missio,* it is clear the presence of the Spirit in other religions does not confer on them an 'independent legitimacy'. This positive judgment on other religions is a Christian theological understanding and relates to the doctrine of the Trinity within the church. He asserts that this understanding makes it different from any pluralistic or inclusivistic interpretation. He stresses the ecclesiological implications of recognising the Spirit's presence in other religions in this document. By being attentive to the working of the Holy Spirit in other religions, not only are the non-Christian religions fulfilled, but Christianity itself also finds her fulfilment. The Spirit working in other religions brings gifts that must be discovered and nurtured by the church.[34]

D'Costa believes this trinitarian approach will be well received by non-Christians (which he calls an 'intra–Christian claim'). In her engagement with non-Christian religions, the church is called to be a sign of forgiving redemption, and she may also receive the gifts of God through other religions. He also makes it clear that the Christian revelation is the ultimate revelation; there will be no new revelation, but a deeper understanding of what was originally received. This means that revealed truth must always be 'deeply penetrated, better understood, and set forth to greater advantage'.[35] There is no question of revelation taking place in other religions: 'All creation, all time and history ... are now taken up into the new creation inaugurated by Jesus'.[36]

---

33 Gavin D'Costa, *The Meeting of Religions and the Trinity* (New York: Orbis Books, Maryknoll, 2000), 111.

34 Ibid., 114.

35 *Gaudium et Spes*, Pastoral Constitution of the Church in the Modern Word (1965), http://www.vatican.va/archive/hist_councils/ii_vatican_council/documents/vat–ii_cons_19651207_gaudium–et–spes_en.html#top, 44.

36 Gavin D'Costa, *The Meeting of Religions and the Trinity* (New York: Orbis Books, Maryknoll, 2000), 129.

To sum up, D' Costa states that the trinitarian doctrine of God within Christianity allows it 'to maintain a real openness to God in history'.[37] God has acted historically through the Incarnation. And thus, the church must acknowledge God's activity outside its own visible confines. This is the theological basis for openness. The history of religions is still in the making and we have no idea about the final outcome, but we must be attentive and open to history. We can only affirm or negate other religions in the historical context of other traditions. By taking other religions seriously, the church is open to genuine change and challenges.

Criticism of D'Costa's Theology of Religions

For many years, D'Costa considered himself as an inclusivist and argued for the threefold typology against its critics. However, in *Christianity and World Religions*, he has opted for what he calls 'universal-access exclusivism' (UAE). However, there is really no difference between his UAE and 'restrictive inclusivism' (RAE), except that in UAE one needs to have specific knowledge of the Gospel to be saved.

D'Costa argues that both the pluralists and inclusivists include an exclusivist logic and thus, even in pluralism, there is this lack of tolerance and openness. Thus pluralism usually collapses into forms of exclusivism. In *The Meeting of Religions and the Trinity*, D'Costa proposes a form of Roman Catholic 'Trinitarian exclusivism' that he believes better embodies, justifies, and articulates the pluralists' goals. He claims that in order to see the Spirit working in other religious traditions, we must attempt to hear the self-understanding of some aspects of those beliefs, and then try to give it a Roman Catholic interpretation. God may speak through other religious traditions.

---

37   Ibid., 133.

142

At the same time, D'Costa also admits that Christ and the Trinity are never the objects of worship in other faiths. Hence, a Roman Catholic understanding of the Holy Spirit at work is not part of the self-understanding of other religions. If there is truth in other religions, it must be truth according to them and not according to Christian interpretation. If that is the case, how can D'Costa's approach satisfy the pluralist's goal? If he does not take the claims of other religions in their own terms, he fails to achieve the aim of the pluralist.

The church's silence in the documents regarding other religions *per se* as salvific structures is an indication that pluralism and inclusivsm are not acceptable, according to D'Costa. By using the various official church proclamations to support his exclusivist position, D'Costa turns out to be nothing more than a spokesman for the *Congregation for the Doctrine of the Faith* (CDF) – the Roman theological watchdog. His 'universal-access exclusivism' contains self-contradictory positions when applied to the 'revelatory' function of non-Christian religions. It would have been better if he had stuck to his initial inclusivist position which reflects better the Catholic Church's stand on non-Christian beliefs. And in some ways, Newman's understanding of the Christian faith and tradition provides a better model for dialogue with non-Christian religions.

Nonetheless, we can relate Newman's teaching on Christianity towards other religions to certain aspects of D'Costa's theology of religions. The idea of non-Christian religions acting as *preparatio evangelica*, the importance of natural law, natural religion, conscience and reason as possible ways to know the one true God had been explored in Newman's writings. With his stress on God's historical engagement with his people, Newman believed the Christian faith can be discerned in the rituals and beliefs of other traditions and he was aware that the beauty of the Christian religion is to be sought not apart from non-Christian beliefs, but in relation to them.

In *The Arians of the Fourth Century*, Newman discusses the relationship between paganism and Christianity, and argues that pagan belief can serve as a preparation for the Gospel of Christ. Thus, his understanding of other religious beliefs reveals a remarkable liberality in that he believes there is something true and divinely revealed in every authentic religion. This comes close to the *restrictivist inclusivist* or *universal-access exclusivist* theology of religions with its stress on God's historical engagement with his people, natural law, conscience, and its acknowledgement of the positive role played by non-Christian religious traditions in the salvation history of mankind.

Legacy of the Enlightenment [38]

Both Newman and D'Costa believe pluralism and the anti-dogmatic principle came about as the result of the Enlightenment. D'Costa labels it as 'liberal modernity', while Newman simply calls it 'liberalism'. The Enlightenment has influenced philosophy, moral and Christian thought since the eighteenth century, and has resulted in diluting Christian practice and message. D'Costa argues that the Enlightenment, in granting equality to all religious beliefs, actually ended denying any truth to any of them.[39] Newman knew that early in his life and expressed it in his *biglietto* speech where he asserts that liberalism in religion teaches that one creed is as good as another; that truth and falsehood in religion are matters of opinion; and that one doctrine is as good as another, as the pluralists believe. Pluralism is a product of liberalism which Newman calls a 'great *apostasia*' and 'is one and the same everywhere'. It is pervasive and is already 'a formidable success' because the liberal principle is forced on us from the necessity of the case'.[40] Here, Newman identifies liberalism with relativism in reli-

---

38   See Chapters 4 and 5 of Alasdair MacIntyre, *After Virtue* (Notre Dame: University of Notre Dame Press, 1984).

39   Gavin D'Costa, *The Meetings of Religions and the Trinity* (New York: Orbis Books, Maryknoll, 2000), 2.

40   *Biglietto Speech*,
     http://www.newmanreader.org/works/addresses/file2.html#biglietto, 67–68.

gious beliefs. But he was also quick to praise its virtues of justice and truthfulness later in his speech.

The 'Enlightenment project', as McIntyre calls it, advocates a conception of rationality divorced from its historical and social contexts, and independent of man's ultimate purpose in life. Liberalism develops from this rationalism and subjects Christian revelation to reason. This approach gives human reason prime importance in revelation and not God himself. This reminds us of Newman's teaching that secular reason has no place in judging the truth or falsity of a religion – this means that we cannot use reason as the sole criteria in evaluating religious belief. For Newman, religion is not just a subjective understanding; the Christian faith for him is a belief in the person of Jesus Christ, an objective truth beyond secular reasoning.

Liberalism advocates the shifting of focus from God to human beings, and Newman believes this would eventually lead to atheism. Religion becomes the fulfilment of man's needs and not the glorification of God. This is what a pluralist like Hick attempts to do in his search for meaning and unity in religious beliefs. The Enlightenment view of rationality demands a clear conception of the divine so that man can control and find fulfilment in it. It is a myth, according to Roland Barthes, this attempt to transform history in 'Essences', to make this world into an object that can be possessed.[41] Newman, on the other hand, has a profound sense of the mystery in Christian revelation.

Echoing Newman, MacIntyre said in an interview in 1994: 'My critique of liberalism is one of the few things that has gone unchanged in my overall view throughout my life. Ever since I understood liberalism, I have wanted nothing to do with it – and that was when I was 17 years old'[42] From his earliest writings, MacIntyre set himself in opposition to the liberal order of modernism. Like Newman before him, and in keeping with his deep belief in the communal and histori-

41   Gavin D'Costa, *The Meetings of Religions and the Trinity* (New York: Orbis Books, Maryknoll, 2000), 26–27.
42   Thomas D'Andrea, *Tradition, Rationality, and Virtue* (Aldershot: Ashgate Publishing Limited, 2006), 109.

cal, he consistently maintains that a non-liberal order would have to draw heavily not only for its critique of liberalism, but also for its positive alternative to liberalism, on sources of which some were plainly pre–modern and others we might today classify as postmodern.

Tradition in MacIntyre's sense is a historical process of reflection that is tied to the practices and institutions of the community, and he holds allegiance to a tradition known as Aristotelian-Thomism. The Aristotelian tradition is attractive to MacIntyre because it is informed by religious experience and aspiration. No matter what its limitation, religion has 'a substantial prima facie claim to wisdom about the human condition'.[43] MacIntyre believes modernity with its attendant individualism, so much part of the liberal order, has been defeated. But liberalism is here to stay – it has not been defeated, but has become stronger than ever. Newman had accepted that fact.

Relationship between Natural Religion and Christianity

Newman's theology of religions is located in *An Essay in Aid of Grammar of Assent* where he explores the relation between natural religion and Christianity by examining five characteristics of providence, prayer, revelation, sacrifice, and the meditative power of saintly people. Natural religion starts off as a natural phenomenon and rises to deeper experiences of the divine. All valid religions started naturally in the concrete experience of daily life, and find their fulfilment in Christianity. Beauty in daily life, for example, is seen as a reflection of the glory and beneficence of the Creator. Food for the body and water's cleansing power find their full meaning in the Eucharist and baptism respectively. The relationship between natural and religious hope finds its expression in Christianity. The Incarnation

---

43   Gary Gutting, *Pragmatic Liberalism and the Critique of Modernity* (Cambridge: Cambridge University Press, 1999), 89.

fulfils our natural hope as Jesus took on human nature, and raises it to a deeper value in the resurrection.

Newman's understanding of natural religion is based on his doctrine of conscience which he believes is a universal phenomenon, a 'mental act' that is part of life like memory, sensation and reasoning – this feeling of 'right and wrong under a special sanction'. He describes this sanction as 'the sense of a particular judgment', prohibitive or hortatory, and attended by certain distinct emotions which are vital to the experience of conscience. Their presence implies that there is a superior invisible being to whom we are related, and it is only an intelligent being and a living object that could excite in us the feeling of remorse or satisfaction which are part of our experience of conscience.[44]

According to Newman, a person's image of God is rooted in his affective life, in his human experience. This image is conditioned by his education and relationship with others, and also his character and circumstances. People who understand the fundamental lessons of natural religion could discern the hand of God guiding them in their moral actions. For Newman, God's providence in human affairs is fundamental to natural religion. Thus, the experience of conscience reveals God as a law giver and one who wills our happiness at the same time because he is a benevolent ruler who wants the best for us.[45]

The individual's sense of God's goodness leads one to hope in spite of one's sinfulness. Indeed when one is confronted with one's moral weakness and inadequacy, hope acquires a new form and we find our strength in him. Newman writes:

> One of the most important effects of Natural Religion on the mind, in preparation for Revealed, is the anticipation which it creates, that a Revelation will be given.... This pre-sentiment is founded on our sense, on the one hand, of the in-

---

44 *An Essay in Aid of a Grammar of Assent,*
    http://www.newmanreader.org/works/grammar/chapter5–1.html, 105–110.
45 Ibid., 118, 117, 402, 114.

finite goodness of God, and, on the other, of our own extreme misery and need—two doctrines which are the primary constituents of Natural Religion.[46]

Thus, for Newman, an integral part of natural religion is the expectation of revelation. This means that the naturally religious person is always seeking God through rites and ceremonies which he seeks to appease the deity.[47]

As far as the rites of paganism were concerned, Newman displays his liberal instinct in his *Apologia* when he writes about the Alexandrian Church which viewed 'pagan literature, philosophy, and mythology, properly understood ...[as] preparation for the Gospel',[48] a theme taken up in Vatican II.

From his readings of the Fathers, Newman came to the conclusion that much of Christian revelation can be found in other religious beliefs, philosophies and cultures, either in part or in entirety:

> [The] doctrine of a Trinity is found both in the East and in the West; so is the ceremony of washing; so is the rite of sacrifice. The doctrine of the Divine Word is Platonic; the doctrine of the Incarnation is Indian; of a divine kingdom is Judaic; of Angels and demons is Magian; the connexion of sin with the body is Gnostic; celibacy is known to Bonze and Talapoin; a sacerdotal order is Egyptian; the idea of a new birth is Chinese and Eleusinian; belief in sacramental virtue is Pythagorean; and honours to the dead are a polytheism.[49]

Henry Hart Milman in his *History of Christianity* seems to infer that these doctrines found in foreign cultures cannot be part of Christianity, but Newman insists that since we find these in Christianity, they are not automatically pagan because from the beginning of time, God has scattered the seeds of truth far and wide; and hence, all philosophies and religions derive their life and vitality from God. Newman

---

46   Ibid., 404– 405, 417– 418.
47   Ibid.
48   *Apologia pro Vita Sua,*
      http://www.newmanreader.org/works/apologia65/chapter1.html, 27.
49   *Essays Critical and Historical,*
      http://www.newmanreader.org/works/essays/volume2/milman2.html, II, 231.

writes: 'So far then from her creed being of doubtful credit because it resembles foreign theologies, we even hold that one special way in which Providence has imparted divine knowledge to us has been by enabling her to draw and collect it together out of the world'.[50]

Idea of Economy and Fulfilment in Christianity

Newman's understanding of how Christianity is related to other religious traditions is connected to his idea of how God makes himself present in the world. Divine presence and action take different forms according to historical circumstances. Kaufman believes a historical approach to theological investigation can enable Christians to appreciate the integrity and meaning of other religious traditions.[51] The idea of 'economy' first used by the Church Fathers is taken up by Newman and developed further to explain the manner of God's working in our universe. 'Economy' helps us to understand the relationship between various religions.

In the Patristic period, the Fathers were trying to understand the relationship between Christianity and pagan religion. Their catechetical aim was to present the Christian message as intellectually respectable to a largely Hellenistic world and to define it in terms of that culture. The Fathers also attempted to evaluate the significance of pagan philosophies for Christianity and to establish a link between Greek philosophy and revelation. Newman was deeply influenced by his reading of the Fathers which enabled him to formulate his own theology of religions:

50   Ibid., II, 232.
51   Gordon D. Kaufman, 'Religious Diversity, Historical Consciousness, and Christian Theology', in *The Myth of Christian Uniqueness*, edited by John Hick and Paul F. Knitter (London: SCM Press Ltd., 1987), 8.

Some portions of their teaching, magnificent in themselves, came like music to my inward ear, as if the response to ideas, which, with little external to encourage them, I had cherished so long. These were based on the mystical or sacramental principle, and spoke of the various Economies or Dispensations of the Eternal. I understood these passages to mean that the exterior world, physical and historical, was but the manifestation to our senses of realities greater than itself. Nature was a parable: Scripture was an allegory: pagan literature, philosophy, and mythology, properly understood, were but a preparation for the Gospel. The Greek poets and sages were in a certain sense prophets; for 'thoughts beyond their thought to those high bards were given'. There had been a directly divine dispensation granted to the Jews; but there had been in some sense a dispensation carried on in favour of the Gentiles. He who had taken the seed of Jacob for His elect people had not therefore cast the rest of mankind out of His sight.[52]

In the Johannine tradition, Justin Martyr taught that the divine Logos was implanted in every age and race; he called the individual seeds of divine truth *Logos spermatikos*. God's purpose was to lead everyone to some knowledge of the truth no matter how obscure. Thus, in a special way, Jesus Christ, the divine logos, had implanted this seeds of divine truth in the hearts and minds of the Greeks so that they could participate in the life of the Logos. Justin wanted to demonstrate the pre–existence of Christ present and active among the Greeks, but it was Clement of Alexandria who taught that these seeds were a preparation for the Gospel.[53]

Newman uses this idea, 'economy', to explore Christianity in relation to natural religion. His conviction is that all great religious traditions manifest a general economic revelation. An 'economy' is like a bridge that helps people mediate among one another. It is a common measure that mediates between people of different cultures and religions. In human understanding, the receiving of the truth occurs only in as full a measure as our minds can admit it. We always see 'the truth under the conditions of thought which human feebleness

52   *Apologia pro Vita Sua,*
     http://www.newmanreader.org/works/apologia65/chapter1.html , 26–27.
53   Francis McGrath, *John Henry Newman: Universal Revelation* (Mulgrave, Victoria: John Garratt Publishing, 1977), 45–46.

imposes', and we are 'obliged to receive information needful to us, through the medium of our existing ideas, and consequently with but a vague apprehension of its subject–matter'.[54] Likewise, St Thomas Aquinas' theology is based fundamentally on the authority of revelation: the philosophical principle of instrumental causality. God reveals and we receive in faith, which is also God's gift to us. But this knowledge is given to us in our human circumstances through other people. Aquinas also asserts that: '*Quid quid recipitur ad modum recipientis recipitur*' – whatever is received is received according to the mode of the receiver.[55]

The idea of the economy from the Patristic Fathers was further developed by Newman in the sense that, while retaining the core Gospel values, Christianity has to be adapted to the culture of the place. It is a pedagogical approach to bring Christianity to unbelievers, but it can also be used to understand Christianity in the context of other religious traditions. In *Apologia*, Newman speaks about 'cautious dispensation':

> As Almighty God did not all at once introduce the Gospel to the world, and thereby gradually prepared men for its profitable reception, so, according to the doctrine of the early Church, it was a duty, for the sake of the heathen among whom they lived, to observe a great reserve and caution in communicating to them the knowledge of 'the whole counsel of God'. This cautious dispensation of the truth, after the manner of a discreet and vigilant steward, is denoted by the word 'economy'. It is a mode of acting which comes under the head of Prudence, one of the four Cardinal Virtues.

He continues in the same passage,

> The principle of the Economy is this; that out of various courses, in religious conduct or statement, all and each allowable antecedently and in themselves,

54   Lee H. Yearley, *The Ideas of Newman* (University Park: The Pennsylvania State University Press, 1978), 33.
55   St Thomas Aquinas, *The Summa Theologica*, http://www.ccel.org/a/aquinas/summa /FP/FP084.html#FPQ84OUTP1, 84:1.

that ought to be taken which is most expedient and most suitable at the time for the object in hand.[56]

In *Arians of the Fourth Century*, Newman describes revelation as an economy:

> What, for instance, is the revelation of general moral laws, their infringement, their tedious victory, the endurance of the wicked, and the 'winking at the times of ignorance', but an 'Economia' of greater truths untold, the best practical communication of them which our minds in their present state will admit? . . . 'Economia' suited to the practical wants of the multitude, as teaching them in the simplest way the active presence of Him, who after all dwells intelligibly, prior to argument, in their heart and conscience?[57]

This idea is exemplified in *disciplina arcani* or secret teaching used by the Church Fathers to spread Christianity to the pagans. The Christian message was adapted selectively to the mindset of the listeners. Ideas that might be misunderstood were concealed, attention was given to the recipient's situation and ability, and hence, 'caution dispensation' means employing an appropriate mean to reach out to those who could not or were not ready to accept the full message of the Gospel. This reminds us of St Paul in 1 Corinthians 3: 1– 2 when he says, 'Brothers, I myself was unable to speak to you as people of the Spirit: I treated you as sensual men, still infants in Christ What I fed you with was milk, not solid food, for you were not ready for it; and indeed, you are still not ready for it since you are still unspiritual'. Accommodation is necessary in a pluralistic society where the general ideas and feelings of people need to be taken into account to facilitate their reception of novel ideas.[58]

---

56 *Apologia pro Vita Sua,*
    http://www.newmanreader.org/works/apologia65/notef.html, 343.
57 *Arians of the Fourth Century,*
    http://www.newmanreader.org/works/arians/chapter1–3.html, 75.
58 See Lee H. Yearley, *The Ideas of Newman* (University Park: The Pennsylvania State University Press, 1978), 35.

Newman acknowledges that non-Christians are included within a general economy of revelation. Secret teaching works because revelation is universal and 'the elementary information given to the heathen or catechumen was in no sense undone by the subsequent secret teaching, which was in fact but the refilling up of a bare but correct outline'.[59] It is crucial to understand his assertion that non-Christian traditions are included within a general economy of revelation: that there were 'various Economies of Dispensations of the Eternal'.[60]

The general revelation in which there is the 'dispensation of paganism' is clear to Newman because he believes all knowledge of religion comes from God alone. There was never a time when God did not speak to his people, and hence, in every religious tradition, there is always some truth and holiness because revelation is universal and not local. Conscience plays a great role in determining the notion of right and wrong, in addition to the guidance provided by tradition, as Newman has argued in *Arians of the Fourth Century*.[61] Religious truths 'have been secretly re–animated and enforced by new communications from the unseen world'. General revelation embraces all great religious traditions. Therefore, Newman asserts that 'there may have been heathen poets and sages, or sibyls again, in a certain extent divinely illuminated, ... [who existed as the] organs through whom religious and moral truth was conveyed to their countrymen'; indeed 'the Sacrifice, which is the hope of Christians, has its power and its success wherever men seek God with their whole heart'.[62]

The Fathers of the Alexandrian Church taught that all humankind will be saved. It was the teaching of Plato that included reincarnation, that influenced the Fathers. Origen believed that not a single rational soul would perish and even the worst sinner will eventually attain salvation. Hellfire punishment is a divine instruction or correction, not an

59   *Apologia pro Vita Sua,*
     http://www.newmanreader.org/works/apologia65/notef.html, 345.
60   Ibid., 27.
61   *Arians of the Fourth Century,*
     http://www.newmanreader.org/works/arians/chapter1–3.html, 80.
62   Ibid., 82.

instrument of eternal torment; souls are essentially rational and they will eventually learn of the truth of the divine pedagogy. *Apokatastasis* (restoration of all things) is the word used by the Fathers to describe universal salvation. Newman was drawn towards Platonism and influenced by the broad philosophy of Clement and Origen as he admits it in *Apologia*.

Although Newman acknowledges that pagans can be saved because of universal revelation, he believes that heretics are excluded from it. Pagans are not men 'in a state of actual perdition but as being in imminent danger of 'the wrath to come' because they are in bondage and ignorance, and probably under God's displeasure, that is, the vast majority of them are so in fact; but not necessarily so, from the very circumstance of their being heathen'.[63]

The idea of economy, according to Newman, leads to the idea of universal revelation, which means that Christianity fulfils and completes natural religion. God the Father slowly teaches his children ideas fitted to their level of maturity and eventually giving the full truth of the Gospel as they grow up. Newman argues that:

> ... the life of Christ brings together and concentrates truths concerning the chief good and the laws of our being, which wander idle and forlorn over the surface of the moral world, and often appear to diverge from each other. It collects the scattered rays of light, which, in the first days of creation, were poured over the whole face of nature, into certain intelligible centres, in the firmament of the heaven.[64]

In 1830, Newman wrote to his brother Charles on revelation which reveals his own understanding of the theology of religions:

> I believe in a universal revelation – the doctrines of which are preserved by tradition in the world at large, in Scripture in the Christian Church. The only difference in this respect between us and the heathen nations, is, that we have a written, they have an unwritten memorial of it...Revelation is a gift, like all

63   Ibid., 84.
64   *Oxford University Sermons*,
       http://www.newmanreader.org/works/oxford/sermon2.html, 27.

154

gifts, diffused with indefinite inequality all over the earth. In the Apostolic Church itself it varies indefinitely in its degree – the Romanists have far less of a revelation than we have. In like manner Islamism in its different forms, and Polytheism besides in its numberless varieties, contain revelation from God – I do not say they are revelations, but they embody revealed truth with more or less clearness and fullness. And this has ever been the case since Noah's time.[65]

Revealed religion, he says, contains doctrines found in Judeo-Christian scripture and they originate from God. However, we are told that 'all knowledge of religion' comes from God, not just revelation, and there has never been a time when God has not spoken and informed us of our duty. In the *Acts of the Apostles*, Paul tells the people that God 'did not leave himself without witness' (14: 17) in the world, and that in every nation he accepts those who fear and obey him. Newman comments:

> It would seem, then, that there is something true and divinely revealed, in every religion all over the earth, overloaded, as it may be, and at times even stifled by the impieties which the corrupt will and understanding of man have incorporated with it. Such are the doctrines of the power and presence of an invisible God, of His moral law and governance, of the obligation of duty, and the certainty of a just judgment, and of reward and punishment, as eventually dispensed to individuals.[66]

Thus, according Newman, revelation is 'a universal, not local gift', and all of us have the guidance of tradition and the sense of what is right and wrong deposited in our conscience. Newman did not condemn heathen beliefs entirely, and he felt that while missionaries opposed idolatrous and immoral activities, they must not reverse the existing order, but lead people to perfection by recovering and purifying the 'essential principles' of the existing belief system. Thus, we do not ridicule or condemn other religions when catechizing. In Newman's opinion, this means that the first step in catechesis is assimilation and not eradication because nobody is completely free of the religious sys-

---

65   Quoted in Francis McGrath, *John Henry Newman: Universal Revelation* (Mulgrave, Victoria: John Garratt Publishing, 1977), 71.
66   Ibid., 71–72.

tem he is born into and anyone who professes even a portion of truth is in a better condition to accept Christianity.[67]

Historical Character of God's Self–Revelation

Newman believes God takes human history seriously and his self-communication does not violate our essential nature as historical and social beings. In other words, God addresses us as we are and engages us on our terms, but at the same time his presence is a mediated and veiled presence:

> If then He is still actively present with His own work, present with nations and with individuals, He must be acting by means of its ordinary system ... He is acting through, with, and beneath those physical, social, and moral laws, of which our experience informs us ... and that, as there is a particular Providence, so of necessity that Providence is secretly concurring and co–operating with that system which meets the eye, and which is commonly recognized among men as existing. It is not too much to say that this is the one great rule on which the Divine Dispensations with mankind have been and are conducted, that the visible world is the instrument, yet the veil, of the world invisible.[68]

In view of this, Newman could affirm in *Arians of the Fourth Century* that the divinity of traditional religions be described as 'dispensation of paganism', and that all knowledge of religion is from God and not just what the Bible teaches. He also insists that God always speaks to his people about his duty, and our conscience is the basis of our experience of the divine. In this work, Newman also discusses in an original and impressive manner the possibility of salvation outside

---

67 Francis McGrath, *John Henry Newman: Universal Revelation* (Mulgrave, Victoria: John Garratt Publishing, 1977), 73.
68 *Essays Critical and Historical*,
http://www.newmanreader.org/works/essays/volume2/milman1.html, II:192.

Christianity and explores the relationship of Christianity to other religions, the issue of revelation in non-Christian religion, with an emphasis on Natural Religion.

For Newman, a religion is essentially a unified system involving the whole person by taking hold of his intellect, heart and will. Merrigan argues that Newman's awareness of this fact goes back to his experience as a tutor at Oriel College when he recognised the importance of moral commitment and devotional practice, after being influenced by John Keble and Hurrell Froude, who convinced him that an ethical disposition was necessary to understanding religious truth because the intellect is the 'handmaid of our moral nature'.[69]

In *Arians of the Fourth Century*, Newman teaches us that religion is a universal phenomenon, understood as a complex of stories, rituals, code of conduct, and one of the first principles is that everyone has a conscience that can lead them to God. Revelation is a universal gift and he turns to the natural religion of paganism instead of the doctrine of *Logos* (which had served the Fathers) because this is more accessible to the non-Christians.

Some argued that if a doctrine has the influence of Platonism, Judaism or paganism, it was not part of Christian revelation. But Newman taught that traces of the Trinity, the Incarnation, and the atonement are found 'among heathens, Jews, and philosophers'. Such sources do not negate Christian revelation, but enhance it:

> ... for the Almighty scattered through the world, before His Son came, vestiges and gleams of His true Religion, and collected all the separated rays together, when He set Him on His holy hill to rule the day, and the Church, as the moon, to govern the night. In the sense in which the doctrine of the Trinity is Platonic, doubtless the doctrine of mysteries generally is Platonic also. But this is by the way. What I have here to notice is, that the same supposed objection can be and has been made against the books of Scripture too, viz., that they borrow from external sources. Unbelievers have accused Moses of borrowing his law from the Egyptians or other Pagans; and elaborate comparisons have been instituted,

69   Terrence Merrigan, 'Christianity and the Non–Christian Religions in the Light of the Theology of John Henry Newman', *Irish Theological Quarterly* 68 (2003), 345.

on the part of believers also, by way of proving it; though even if proved, and so far as proved, it would show nothing more than this,—that God, who gave His law to Israel absolutely and openly, had already given some portions of it to the heathen.[70]

As an empiricist, Newman prefers to concentrate on the concrete historical fact of the economy of salvation. Merrigan says this option for history led Newman to value non-Christian religions as an instrument of God's saving work.[71] In *The Idea of a University*, Newman writes as follows:

> He [God] introduces Himself, He all but concurs, according to His good pleasure, and in His selected season, in the issues of unbelief, superstition, and false worship, and He changes the character of acts by His overruling operation. He condescends, though He gives no sanction, to the altars and shrines of imposture, and He makes His own fiat the substitute for its sorceries. He speaks amid the incantations of Balaam, raises Samuel's spirit in the witch's cavern, prophesies of the Messiah by the tongue of the Sibyl ... and baptizes by the hand of the misbeliever.[72]

Hans Küng also asserts that 'when one compares Christianity with the religions of Indian origin, above all Hinduism and Buddhism, they all seem at least to share various words, usages, myths, and ideas of the Indo European language group between the Ganges and the Mediterranean'. Küng also argues that 'the Chinese religions are not some kind of Far Eastern and exotic appendage of general religious history, to be treated as marginal or as an afterthought….the Chinese religions must be taken seriously as a third independent religious river system,

---

70   *Discussions and Arguments*,
     http://www.newmanreader.org/works/arguments/Scripture/lecture6.html, 211.
71   Terrence Merrigan, 'Christianity and the Non–Christian Religions in the Light of the Theology of John Henry Newman', *Irish Theological Quarterly* 68 (2003), 347.
72   *The Idea of a University*,
     http://www.newmanreader.org/works/idea/discourse3.html, 65–66.

equal in value to others'.[73] In his magisterial book, *Towards a Christian Theology of Religious Pluralism*, Jacque Dupuis argues that 'the religions of the world are various 'faces' or expressions of human religious experience, which is at once one and manifold'.[74]

Newman's recognition of the centrality of Christ did not prevent him from appreciating the whole religious history of mankind, and he was willing to acknowledge that some of the features in Christianity have parallels in non-Christian religions as he observes that 'When Providence would make a Revelation, He does not begin anew, but uses the existing system ... Thus the great characteristic of Revelation is addition, substitution'.[75]

In *An Essay on Development of Christian Doctrine*, Newman writes about Christianity's ability to assimilate ideas and practices from other religious traditions without sacrificing truths and goodness already contained in them. He believes that all religious systems possess the 'same great and comprehensive subject matter', and from the beginning, Christianity was influenced by 'rites, sects, and philosophies, which contemplated the same questions, advocated the same truths', and 'wore the same external appearance'.[76] Christians referred all truth and revelation to the supreme God – this is the cardinal distinction between Christianity and other religions according to Newman. In spite of two thousand years of 'collision and conflict', the Gospel has succeeded in 'purifying, assimilating, transmuting, and taking into itself the many–coloured beliefs, forms of worship, codes of duty, schools of thought, through which it was ever moving. It was Grace, and it was Truth'.[77]

---

73   Hans Küng and Julia Ching, *Christianity and Chinese Religions* (London: SCM Press, 1988), xi –xii.
74   Jacques Dupuis S.J., *Toward A Christian Theology of Religious Pluralism* (New York: Orbis Book, 1997), 3.
75   *Essays Critical and Historical*, http://www.newmanreader.org/works/essays/volume2/milman1.html,II:194195.
76   *An Essay on the Development of the Christian Doctrine*, http://www. newmanreader.org/works/development/chapter8.html, 355.
77   Ibid., 357.

Thus, Christianity differs from other religions not in kind or nature, but in its characteristics, origins and in the gifts of the Holy Spirit:

> True religion is the summit and perfection of false religions; it combines in one whatever there is of good and true separately remaining in each. And in like manner the Catholic Creed is for the most part the combination of separate truths.... So that, in matter of fact, if a religious mind were educated in and sincerely attached to some form of heathenism or heresy, and then were brought under the light of truth, it would be drawn off from error into the truth, not by losing what it had, but by gaining what it had not, not by being unclothed, but by being 'clothed upon'...That same principle of faith which attaches it at first to the wrong doctrine would attach it to the truth; and that portion of its original doctrine, which was to be cast off as absolutely false, would not be directly rejected, but indirectly, in the reception of the truth which is its opposite. True conversion is ever of a positive, not a negative character'.[78]

Christianity, because of its continuity and the firmness of her principles, has succeeded in assimilating ideas which other religions find incompatible to their own traditions. The early church had no difficulty accepting Gnostic and Platonic ideas found in St John's Gospel. She confidently adapts 'the very instruments and appendages of demon–worship to an evangelical use' and she already had 'the archetypes on which other religions had modelled their ideas and practice'.[79]

Newman and Post-Conciliar Teaching

The idea that God might use non-Christian forms of religious practice to carry out his saving mission is a post-conciliar teaching, and New-

---

78   Ibid., 200–201.
79   Francis McGrath, *John Henry Newman: Universal Revelation* (Mulgrave, Victoria: John Garratt Publishing, 1977), 80.

man's reflection on this issue suggest that he was the 'invisible *peritus*' of the Second Vatican Council as Paul VI had described him.[80] It may well be that Newman was one of the first to understand the significance of religious plurality although he was limited in his knowledge of other religious traditions. We are aware now that there are many religious traditions – Buddhism, Hinduism, and Confucianism, for example – that have contributed to the improvement of the lives of their adherents. These religious traditions and various forms of secular humanism also have 'quite impressive resources for interpreting and orienting human existence and for giving significant formation to human individual and social life'.[81]

Newman was aware that mankind always has the guidance of tradition. In fact he thinks that men should learn to know themselves, and contemplate God's divine nature through the tutelage of the law and natural religion before they can understand the full implications of the Gospel. Otherwise they can become fundamentalists or fanatics. In *Arians of the Fourth Century*, Newman writes:

---

80   Terrence Merrigan, 'The Anthropology of Conversion: Newman and the Contemporary Theology of Religions', in *Newman and Conversion*, edited by Ian Ker (Edinburgh: T& T Clarke, 1997), 117. Avery Dulles even claims that Newman was in some ways ahead of Vatican II in the way he grappled with certain questions that the council did not foresee. See Avery Dulles, 'Newman's Ecclesiology' in *Newman after a Hundred Years*, edited by Ian Ker and Alan G. Hill (Oxford: Clarendon Press, 1990), 398. Nicholas Lash maintains that the things Newman advocated became a reality at Vatican II – 'freedom, the supremacy of conscience, the Church as a communion, a return to Scripture and the fathers, the rightful place of the laity, work for unity, and all the efforts to meet the needs of the age, and for the Church to take its place in the modern world'. In short, Newman was a 'progressive'. At the same time Newman was against a liberalism that 'knows nothing of the otherness of God or of obedience to his will'. As a 'theologian of Grace', Newman possessed an 'intense awareness of God and the unseen world'. See Nicholas Lash, 'Tides and Twilight: Newman since Vatican II ' in *Newman after a Hundred Years*, edited by Ian Ker and Alan G. Hill (Oxford: Clarendon Press, 1990), 460-461.

81   Gordon D. Kaufman, 'Religious Diversity, Historical Consciousness, and Christian Theology', in *The Myth of Christian Uniqueness*, edited by John Hick and Paul F. Knitter (London: SCM Press Ltd., 1987), 4.

... much of that mischievous fanaticism is avoided, which at present abounds from the vanity of men, who think that they can explain the sublime doctrines and exuberant promises of the Gospel, before they have yet learned to know themselves and to discern the holiness of God, under the preparatory discipline of the Law and of Natural Religion. Influenced, as we may suppose, by these various considerations, from reverence for the free spirit of Christian faith, and still more for the sacred truths which are the objects of it, and again from tenderness both for the heathen and the neophyte, who were unequal to the reception of the strong meat of the full Gospel, the rulers of the Church were dilatory in applying a remedy, which nevertheless the circumstances of the times imperatively required.[82]

Not a fundamentalist, but an open-minded person with a liberal temper, Newman was prepared to accept truths that can be found in other religious traditions, and to modify and accommodate his opinions when necessary. In *Essay on the Development of Christian Doctrine*, he asserts that:

For three hundred years the documents and the facts of Christianity have been exposed to a jealous scrutiny; works have been judged spurious which once were received without a question; facts have been discarded or modified which were once first principles in argument; new facts and new principles have been brought to light; philosophical views and polemical discussions of various tendencies have been maintained with more or less success.[83]

This is considered one of Newman's great theological contributions, parallel to Darwin's *Origin of Species*. He looks to St Paul who was able to relate Christianity to the idolatries he found in Athens:

In what sense can it be said, that there is any connection between Paganism and Christianity so real, as to warrant the preacher of the latter to conciliate idolaters by allusion to it? St Paul evidently connects the true religion with the existing systems which he laboured to supplant, in his speech to the Athenians in the Acts, and his example is a sufficient guide to missionaries now, and a full justi-

82   *Arians of the Fourth Century*,
     http://www.newmanreader.org/works/arians/chapter1–2.html, 37.
83   *An Essay on the Development of the Christian Doctrine*,
     http://www. new manreader.org/ works/development/introduction.html, 30.

fication of the line of conduct pursued by the Alexandrians, in the instances similar to it . . . .[84]

This is prophetic indeed, as the teaching of Vatican II and thereafter proved that Newman was ahead of his times. Without actually using the term, he was already speaking of the concept of inculturation in the new evangelization. John Paul II in *Redemptoris Missio* teaches:

> Through inculturation the Church makes the Gospel incarnate in different cultures and at the same time introduces peoples, together with their cultures, into her own community. She transmits to them her own values, at the same time taking the good elements that already exist in them and renewing them from within. Through inculturation the Church, for her part, becomes a more intelligible sign of what she is, and a more effective instrument of mission.[85]

Newman believes there is something true and divinely revealed in every authentic religion, although at times it is stifled by impieties which corrupt the will and understanding of man. Hence, a Christian missionary, according to him, 'believing God's hand to be in every system, so far forth as it is true . . . will, after St Paul's manner, seek some points in the existing superstitions as the basis of his own instructions, instead of indiscriminately condemning and discarding the whole assemblage of heathen opinions and practices ...'.[86]

In line with Newman's teaching in *Arians of the Fourth Century*, the possibility of salvation is extended to the whole world. John Paul II reiterated this teaching in his encyclical, *Redemptor Hominis* (1979) by asserting that 'man – every man without any exception whatever – has been redeemed by Christ, and because with man – with each man without any exception whatever – Christ is in a way united, even

---

84   *Arians of the Fourth Century*,
      http://www.newmanreader.org/works/arians/chapter1-3.html,79.
85   John Paul II, *Redemptoris Missio*, 'On the permanent validity of the Church's missionary mandate' (1990),
      http://www.vatican.va/edocs/ENG0219/__P7.HTM, 52.
86   *Arians of the Fourth Century*,
      http://www.newmanreader.org/works/arians/chapter1–3.html, 84.

when man is unaware of it'.[87] The Roman Catholic Church rejects nothing which is true and holy in other religious traditions.

Friedrich Max Müller, a pioneer in comparative study of religions in the nineteenth century, sent Newman a copy of his book, *Introduction to the Science of Religion*, which suggests the idea that 'all religions are different dialects of an unknown common language'.[88] Christian dogma may just be the 'stammering of a child', but God would 'translate the faltering utterances of all his children, even those … we condemn because we do not understand them'.[89] Newman was no pluralist, but he recognised that this field of comparative study of religions 'opens upon the mind speculations wonderfully attractive and beautiful' and he believed these dogmas would eventually bear testimony to the fact of Christian revelation.[90]

Otto Karrer, a German theologian in the 1930s, argued that Christian apologetics must be prepared to see with clarity what is good and what is not so good in any religion, and to evaluate it with equal honesty.[91] In writing on the Alexandrian doctrine of the *Logos*, Hans Urs von Balthazar suggests that the 'adoption and Christianization of pagan wisdom' is no 'profanation of divine wisdom', but the 'harvesting of what belonged originally to the true *Logos*'. All philosophy, mythology, and poetry belonged to Christ and then to the people.[92] Karl Rahner asserts that prior to God's self-revelation in Jesus Christ, there already existed the presence of God in the heart and mind of every individual – 'a presence in the form of a question to which Jesus is the ultimate answer'.[93]

87 *Redemptor Hominis* (1979).
    http://www.vatican.va/holy_father/john_paul_ii/encyclicals/documents/hf_jp–
    ii_enc_04031979_redemptor–hominis_en.html, 14.
88 Francis McGrath, *John Henry Newman: Universal Revelation* (Mulgrave, Victoria: John Garratt Publishing, 1977), 93.
89 Quoted in Francis McGrath, *John Henry Newman: Universal Revelation* (Mulgrave, Victoria: John Garratt Publishing, 1977), 93.
90 Ibid.
91 Ibid., 147.
92 Ibid., 148.
93 Ibid., 149.

Doubtless many bishops and theologians, including Joseph Ratzinger at the Second Vatican Council were influenced by Newman directly or indirectly. His insights into many theological issues including the theology of religions are still relevant in present-day society. Newman would surely endorse this teaching of the Council:

> Those also can attain to salvation who through no fault of their own do not know the Gospel of Christ or His Church, yet sincerely seek God and moved by grace strive by their deeds to do His will as it is known to them through the dictates of conscience. Nor does Divine Providence deny the helps necessary for salvation to those who, without blame on their part, have not yet arrived at an explicit knowledge of God and with His grace strive to live a good life. Whatever good or truth is found amongst them is looked upon by the Church as a preparation for the Gospel. She knows that it is given by Him who enlightens all men so that they may finally have life.[94]

---

94 *Lumen Gentium, Dogmatic Constitution on the Church* (1964),
http://www.vatican.va/archive/hist_councils/iivatican_council/documents/vat–
iiconst1964 1121lumen–gentiumen.html, 16.

Conclusion

In his visit to the United Kingdom in September 2010 to beatify Newman, Ratzinger as Pope Benedict XVI urged Britain to maintain its respect for religious traditions and warned against 'aggressive forms of secularism'. He said, 'Today, the United Kingdom strives to be a modern and multicultural society ... in this challenging enterprise, may it always maintain its respect for those traditional values and cultural expressions that more aggressive forms of secularism no longer value or even tolerate'.[1]

It is well known that Ratzinger has always been concerned with the threat of aggressive secularism as evident in his writings and addresses. His preoccupation with this intractable problem was not so much a reactionary stance as it was the position of a priest deeply concerned with the secularization not only of Western society, but of the church itself. In an address to the plenary members of the Council for Culture, 'The Church and the challenge of secularization', Ratzinger says:

---

1   *The Telegraph*, http://www.telegraph.co.uk/news/newstopics/religion/the-pope /8006272/Pope-Benedict-XVI-warns-against-aggressive-secularism-in-Britain .html. Ratzinger believed that truth, which should have re-energized Europe, was denied. This was in reference to the European constitutional treaty signed in October 2004. According to George Weigel, 'the drafters of Europe's new constitution were determined ... to declare secularism – and the scepticism and relativism that inform secularism – as the official creed ... of the newly expanded European Union'. To mention the historical cultural contributions of Christianity to a Europe committed to freedom, human rights and democracy in the preamble would be to acknowledge that freedom and the spiritual dimension of the human experience were related. This is what the drafters of Europe's constitution were determined to avoid. George Weigel, *God's Choice* (New York: HarperCollins Publishers, 2005), 221.

Secularization, which presents itself in cultures by imposing a world and humanity without reference to Transcendence, is invading every aspect of daily life and developing a mentality in which God is effectively absent, wholly or partially, from human life and awareness. This secularization is not only an external threat to believers, but has been manifest for some time in the heart of the Church herself. It profoundly distorts the Christian faith from within, and consequently, the lifestyle and daily behaviour of believers. They live in the world and are often marked, if not conditioned, by the cultural imagery that impresses contradictory and impelling models regarding the practical denial of God: there is no longer any need for God, to think of him or to return to him. Furthermore, the prevalent hedonistic and consumer mindset fosters in the faithful and in pastors a tendency to superficiality and selfishness that is harmful to ecclesial life.[2]

Ratzinger has always had a great interest in Newman.[3] When he spoke of the small boat of Christian thought being tossed about on the waves of the ideological currents, many people thought these remarks too pessimistic, but Ratzinger knew what he was speaking about. His homily to the College of Cardinals on 18 April 2005 at the mass on the dictatorship of relativism echoes Newman's *biglietto* speech at the Palazzo della Pigna on 12 May 1879, when Newman received the formal message that Leo XIII would make him cardinal. Ratzinger says,

---

2   Pope Benedict XVI, 'The Church and the challenge of secularization', *Christ to the World 53*, no. 5 (September 2008), 390. Gary D. Glenn says that the natural consequence for Europe's abandoning Christianity for liberal secularism is that it has become Muslim. Perhaps Heidegger was right when he said, 'Only a god can save us'. See Gary D. Glenn, 'Is secularism the end of liberalism? : reflections on Europe's demographic decline drawing on Pope Benedict, Habermas, Nietzsche and Strauss', *Catholic Social Science Review* 13, (2008), 92.

3   When Ratzinger joined the seminary in Freising in 1946, his Prefect of Studies, Alfred Läpple, who had a great influence on him, was working on a dissertation on conscience in the work of Newman. Ratzinger has said that for seminarians of his generation, "Newman's teaching on conscience became an important foundation for theological personalism, which was drawing us all in its sway. Our image of the human being as well as our image of the Church was permeated by this point of departure." Quoted by Tracey Rowland in "The Influence of John Henry Newman in Benedict XVI," *ABC*, http://www.abc.net.au/religion/articles/2010/09/16/3013343.htm.

How many winds of doctrine we have known in recent decades, how many ideological currents, how many ways of thinking... The small boat of thought of many Christians has often been tossed about by these waves – thrown from one extreme to the other: from Marxism to liberalism, even to libertinism; from collectivism to radical individualism; from atheism to a vague religious mysticism; from agnosticism to syncretism, and so forth ... Having a clear faith, based on the creed of the Church, is often labelled today as a fundamentalism. Whereas relativism, which is letting oneself be tossed and 'swept along by every wind of teaching' [Ephesians 4:14] looks like the only attitude acceptable to today's standards. We are moving towards a dictatorship of relativism which does not recognize anything as for certain and which has as its highest goal one's own ego and one's own desires.[4]

Relativism does not bring freedom; it enslaves and put people at the mercy of those in power. Ratzinger concerns bring to mind a sermon Newman preached in 1873, 'The Infidelity of the Future'. Christianity has never yet had experience of a world simply irreligious, but Newman foresaw a time when Christianity would be a minority religion and the general culture of faith greatly weakened. He anticipated a time when people in Europe would no longer believe. What Newman foresaw, we now recognise:

I am speaking of evils, which in their intensity and breadth are peculiar to these times. But I have not yet spoken of the root of all these falsehoods—the root as it ever has been, but hidden; but in this age exposed to view and unblushingly avowed—I mean, that spirit of infidelity itself which I began by referring to as the great evil of our times, though of course when I spoke of the practical force of the objections which we constantly hear and shall hear made to Christianity, I showed it is from this spirit that they gain their plausibility.[5]

4   'Cardinal Ratzinger's Homily', *Vatican Radio*,
      http://storico.radiovaticana.org/en1/storico/2005-04/33987.html.
5   'The Infidelity of the Future', Opening of St. Bernard's Seminary, 2nd October 1873,
      http://www.newmanreader.org/works/ninesermons/sermon9.html.

The situation Newman anticipated has much in common with the postmodern condition in our contemporary secular society which gives rise to relativism. [6]

There are similarities between the teachings of Ratzinger and Newman and a common thread uniting their thought – their aversion to the tyranny of liberalism which is a product of the modern secular society. Since World War II, Ratzinger has experienced what Newman had predicted: the consequences when revealed religion is not recognised as true and objective, and where religious beliefs is but a private affair for people. What worried Newman in the nineteenth century also worried Ratzinger today.

One of Christianity's greatest challenges in its two thousand year history is liberalism in the form of secular reason. It is a threat similar in scope and danger to Gnosticism or Arianism. The ancient heresies are actually an old problem of understanding the Christian faith in a different cultural context; in this case Hellenism. The initial success of Christianity in the West could be attributed to its ability to incorporate from the best of Hellenistic culture.[7]

The political and cultural spheres in the West have been dominated by liberal ideology since the fall of communism, and some Christian thinkers believe this ideology poses a threat to both the freedom and future of the church. Liberalism, also known as the 'Enlight-

6   Frederic Jameson in his foreword to François Lyotard, *The Postmodern Condition* (Manchester: Manchester University Press, 1984) states that postmodernism is understood as involving 'a radical break, both with a dominant culture and aesthetic ….' It has been variously called media society, 'the society of the spectacle', consumer society, the 'bureaucratic society of controlled consumption', or 'postindustrial society' (vii). See also Joseph Natoli and Johannes Willem Bertens, eds., Postmodernism: The Key Figures (Malden, Mass.: Blackwell, 2002), Johannes Willem Bertens, *The Idea of the Postmodern: A History* (New York: Routledge, 1995), Christopher Butler, *Postmodernism: A Very Short Introduction* (Oxford: Oxford University Press, 2002) and Gianni Vattimo, *The Transparent Society* (Baltimore: Johns Hopkins University Press, 1992).
7   Francisco Javier Martínez, "Beyond Secular Reason': Some Contemporary Challenges for the Life and Thought of the Church,' *Communio* 31 (Winter 2004): 557-558.

enment', or 'Modernity', attempts to present an ideal world by rejecting and replacing religion, especially Christianity; and has since become the mainstream culture of the West. The Catholic Church is still trying to deal with the impact of modernity and secularism; the church is also anxious to protect religious freedom for itself and other religions as well based on revelation and reason. Its conflict with modernity is more on an ideological rather than practical level.[8]

Gavin Hyman argues that modern liberalism played a positive role in bringing out Christian ethical teachings which had been obscured along the way. John Milbank acknowledges this when he says 'the attitude towards "secular reason" is never as negative as it appears to be on the surface ... I regard Catholic Christianity as fulfilling the best pagan impulses . . . It follows that there remains truth in all these distortions'.[9] Francis George also maintains that the Enlightenment has many positive aspects, and thus, 'the challenge for the Church lay in distinguishing the erroneous aspects of modernity from those that were compatible with, and even developments of, the Christian faith'.[10]

Obviously, liberalism has its positive and negative aspects. It does not simply distort Christian truths, but can actually help to articulate them. Liberalism gives primacy to individual freedom and derives from it other political principles such as justice, rights, and community. However, 'secular liberalism' is that strand of liberalism which construes individual freedom in strictly secularist terms, rooted solely in the moral and spiritual autonomy of human beings.[11] This led many

8   Gavin D' Costa, *Christianity and World Religions* (Oxford: Wilkey-Blackwell, 2009), 135.
9   Quoted in Gavin Hyman, 'Post Modern Theology and Modern Liberalism,' *Theology Today* 65 (2009): 470.
10   Francis George, 'How Liberalism Fails The Church,' *Commonweal* 24 (November 19, 1999): 26.
11   Jonathan Chaplin, 'Rejecting Neutrality, Respecting Diversity: From 'Liberal Pluralism' to 'Christian Pluralism,'' *Christian Scholar's Review* 35, no.   2 (Winter 2006):145.

Christian thinkers, including Newman and Pope Benedict XVI, to oppose it.

We can also view liberalism as an intellectual heir of the Christian faith from which values like freedom and human dignity – values that we take for granted in our society – are derived. Christianity is able to embrace whatever truth is contained in secular reason. Secular critiques of religion advanced by Feuerbach, Marx, Durkheim, or Nietzsche would not have developed outside Christian soil.[12]

By the early 1800s, the church was besieged by ideas of the Enlightenment or modernity, which in some ways she unwittingly helped to create. This movement has positive aspects because of its stress on liberty, the dignity of the human person and values, using Kant's formulation: persons are to be treated not as mere means, but as an end. All humans ought to be free from coercion by other humans. The emphasis on each individual's freedom from being manipulated or used by others is the first strand of modernity which is also known as 'liberalism'.[13] The Enlightenment celebrated the universal dignity and rights of the individual, and a commitment to the moral perfection of the world. It developed a scepticism towards traditional ethics and a supreme confidence in reason and science as the primary means to improve life in this world. From the Reformation and its consequent religious pluralism, it eventually developed into the secularization of society.[14]

The church's first historical encounter with the liberalism of the Enlightenment project was the French Revolution, where the state controlled religion and suppressed the church. Naturally the church adopted a negative attitude towards this ideology. Newman and other Liberal Catholics such as Lacordaire, Döllinger, and Acton, rejected certain cultural aspects of modernity, particularly materialism, secu-

---

12 Francisco Javier Martínez, "Beyond Secular Reason': Some Contemporary Challenges for the Life and Thought of the Church,' *Communio* 31 (Winter 2004): 572.

13 Francis George, 'How Liberalism Fails The Church,' *Commonweal* 24 (November 19, 1999): 26.

14 Ibid.

larism, moral relativism and individualism.[15] They also shared the conviction that only a unified and engaging church could solve this cultural crisis by embracing liberal political and economic institutions rather than by rejecting them outright.[16] The church was also indebted to the early liberal Catholics for restoring to the centre of the church's consciousness the Gospel's message that Christ set us free; for giving her the insight and analysis that freed her from her own conservative structure in which she was enclosed, and helped her to reach out to the world.[17]

Not all liberal thought is secular, and Christian and liberal political thought have influenced each other through history in complex associations. There are some who believe the Christian faith is incompatible with liberalism: it 'threatens the integrity of Christianity, because it poisons at its source the meaning of autonomy'.[18] Others maintain the possibility of accommodating many elements of liberalism with Catholic social thought as long as they do not contradict Christian moral principles.[19] They believe liberalism has provided a useful social framework so that the Gospel can advance to protect the dignity of the person. Pope John Paul II believed liberalism could be 'the condition for the Church to invite free persons to live in the communion of Christ and His Mystical Body, which communion is indefinitely deeper, richer, and fuller than the liberal social order'.[20] The point he was making was that liberalism is not the content, but the condition in which the church's message could be promoted.

The intellectual merit of liberalism includes the goal to establish the equality of all people before the law. While it is true certain liberal

---

15   Ibid.
16   Ibid., 27.
17   Ibid., 28.
18   Quoted in Michel Therrien, 'John Paul II's Use of the Term 'Neo-liberalism' in *Ecclesia in America*,' *Josephinum Journal of Theology* 8, no.2 (2001):135.
19   Michel Therrien, 'John Paul II's Use of the Term 'Neo-liberalism' in *Ecclesia in America*,' *Josephinum Journal of Theology* 8, no.2 (2001):135.
20   Quoted in Michel Therrien, 'John Paul II's Use of the Term 'Neo-liberalism' in *Ecclesia in America*,' *Josephinum Journal of Theology* 8, no.2 (2001):136.

excesses have historically led to bloody revolutions and the rejection of legitimate authority, the liberal movement started as an honest attempt to bring an end to the conflict that plagued Europe after the Reformation. Liberals had tried to resolve the social intolerance that was tearing Europe apart by trying to establish a culture founded upon the idea of civil liberty and the doctrine of political pluralism devoid of divisive religious ideologies. They desired to forge a cultural milieu characterised by civil liberty and respect for individual human rights, and to abolish the inequalities of the feudal system.[21]

Certain elements of liberalism situated in a Christian philosophical and theological framework have been recognised and approved by the church: the rights of the individual within a proper anthropology. The church has also condemned the excesses and abuses of liberalism – the 'errors of atomistic individualism, the *absolute* right to private property, the idea that law originates from the will of the people, and the rejection of legitimate authority, especially the authority of the Church'.[22] These are specific errors of liberalism that the church opposes, but she also supports the positive insights that liberalism has to offer, including freedom in the religious, social and economic spheres.

In fact liberalism has given impetus to the church to reflect deeply on human freedom and to develop her social doctrine.[23] Civil liberty provided under the rule of law is of prime importance in any democratic society. But this freedom must be grounded in the moral order. Lord Acton states that 'Liberty has not subsisted outside of Christianity ... freedom should be religious, and that religion should be free'.[24]

Newman attempted to describe the kind of society that was developing and with which the church must learn to cope. This is the society we are familiar with – the decline in Christian belief in west-

---

21 Michel Therrien, 'John Paul II's Use of the Term 'Neo-liberalism' in *Ecclesia in America*,' *Josephinum Journal of Theology* 8, no.2 (2001):136.
22 Ibid., 137.
23 Ibid., 142.
24 Quoted in Michel Therrien, 'John Paul II's Use of the Term 'Neo-liberalism' in *Ecclesia in America*,' *Josephinum Journal of Theology* 8, no.2 (2001):142.

ern countries, the setbacks caused by scandals in the church, and a consumerist culture influenced by the media which resulted in shallow thinking. In this last point, Newman writes, 'This general intelligence of every class of society, general but shallow, is the means of circulating all through the population all the misrepresentations which the enemies of the Church make of her faith and her teaching'.[25]

Newman knew liberalism or secular reason has the chameleon ability to disguise and present itself as the natural way, the way things have always been and should always be. This was made clear in his celebrated *biglietto* speech. The context of his understanding of liberalism is relativism. When we abandon truth, we abandon freedom because only the truth can set us free. If we cannot safeguard objective truth, we only have the 'truth' which those in power decide – tolerance is lost. Hence, when we abandon objective truth, we lose our freedom and society slides into totalitarianism.[26] When revealed religion is not recognised as true, the consequence is the 'dictatorship of relativism' where everything is subjective and private individual judgment becomes the norm.[27] This is the kind of liberalism Newman opposed and his commitment to the dogmatic principle remained constant throughout his life.

Nonetheless, Newman possessed that distinct liberal attribute characterised by an openness and relentless search for truth and freedom. Compared with Keble, Newman was a liberal in that he was actually trying to find a rational basis for dogma, and not just accepting it upon authority. Keble, the quintessential non-liberal, was a man who let himself be guided by authority, but Newman liked to investigate and inquire into the nature of things, as he says, 'I felt then, and

---

25 *Faith and Prejudice*, 'The Infidelity of the Future,'
http://www.newmanreader.org/works/ninesermons/sermon9.html, 121.
26 Roderick Strange, *John Henry Newman: A Mind Alive* (London: Darton, Longman and Todd Ltd., 2008), 45-46.
27 Paul Knitter challenges Joseph Ratzinger by asking 'Where's the 'dictatorship of relativism'?'
http://unionindialogue.org/paulknitter/2010/03/28/wheres-the-dictatorship-of-relativism/.

all along felt, that there was an intellectual cowardice in not finding a basis in reason for my belief, and a moral cowardice in now avowing that basis'.[28] And again he says, 'Few minds in earnest can remain at ease without some sort of rational grounds for their religious belief; to reconcile theory and facts is almost an instinct of the mind'.[29]

Hastings has made a keen observation when he asserts that Newman, by defending a high view on the content of dogma against those liberals who had a low opinion of dogma, was becoming a liberal himself - he had to find a rational basis for his belief in dogma. Paradoxically, it was only after he became a Catholic, and not before, that this rational liberal dimension of Newman's thinking took shape.[30]

Newman's negative judgment on modern culture and society was insightful and correct, and it indicated he was against the liberal spirit in religion. At the same time he benefitted from the liberal atmosphere and the temporal advantages of the age he lived in. His defection to Rome would have been unthinkable in an earlier century, but by 1845, English society was becoming more tolerant and pluralistic.

As mentioned earlier in Chapter 1, Newman asserts that 'this liberal principle is forced on us through the necessity of the case'[31] which means that with the advancement of pluralism of religious belief, together with all that is good and true in liberalism must be accepted as the only option. He sees the intellectual advancement of liberalism as part and parcel of social change.

In the *Letter to the Duke of Norfolk* entitled 'The Encyclical of 1864', Newman stresses the advancement of this new civilization, this great revolution which is the ascendancy of liberalism - an intellectual, religious and social phenomenon which is inevitable. He ex-

---

28   *Apologia pro Vita Sua*,
      http://www.newmanreader.org/works/apologia65/chapter2.html, 66.
29   Ibid., http://www.newmanreader.org/works/apologia65/chapter5.html, 260.
30   Adrian Hastings, *The Theology of a Protestant Catholic* (Philadelphia: Trinity Press International, 1990), 123.
31   *Biglietto speech*,
      http://www.newmanreader.org/ works/ addresses/file2.html#biglietto, 67.

plains, 'When the intellect is cultivated, it is as certain that it will develop into a thousand various shapes, as that infinite hues and tints and shades of colour will be reflected from the earth's surface, when the sunlight touches it; and in matters of religion the more, by reason of the extreme subtlety and abstruseness of the mental action by which they are determined'.[32] He remarks that the whole theory of Toryism fell apart and went the way of all flesh. It was inevitable and not a 'hundred Popes' could stop this flood.[33]

Liberalism in the above context, thus, was a quiet revolution of the nineteenth century where society accepted pluralism and secularism as the nature of things, and as a result, religion began to play a less important role and eventually became a private affair. Newman understood it was futile to fight against this secularising trend even with the help of the political and ecclesiastical authorities.

At the same time Newman saw that as religion lost its public and political influence, it appeared to lose its objective and dogmatic sense as well – it became a private possession controlled by the individual's whims and fancies. Given this state of affairs, it is hard to disagree with Newman's analysis and use of the word 'liberalism' to describe the situation. In fact, with the advantage of time and the advance of knowledge, we realise that Newman was farsighted, insightful and holistic in his view of modern society – he was able to encapsulate a vast process that he was observing all his life.

Newman was aware that the old world was passing away, giving way to the new. In his twenties he was influenced by the liberal view. Later he fought against it as a Tory anti-liberal, but as Hastings observes, the more he fought against it, the more he found himself infatuated by it because he had a lot in common with what liberalism stands for: the love of freedom, the use of reason and the importance of historical science.[34] As a Catholic, he recognised that the old sys-

---

32   *Letter to the Duke of Norfolk,* http://www.newmanreader.org/ works/Anglicans /volume2/gladstone/ section6.html, 267.
33   Ibid., 268.
34   Adrian Hastings, *The Theology of a Protestant Catholic* (Philadelphia: Trinity Press International, 1990), 131.

tem in England was collapsing with the separation of church and state, and liberalism had become the air that nineteenth century men breathed. Newman also recognised that the Catholic Church also needed to breathe this liberal air.

It was Newman's balanced view of liberalism, the integrity of his faith, and the profundity of his judgment that enabled him to influence liberal Catholicism. He was able to reconcile the claims of dogma with the nineteenth century claims for liberty because of his intellectual openness. He possessed a mind of exceptional force and clarity that was caught up on both sides 'in that awful, never-dying duel ... of Authority and Private Judgment alternately advancing and retreating as the ebb and flow of the tide'.[35]

An objective assessment of the significance of Newman's thought is hampered by the movement for his canonization, and any criticism of his life and works is seen as a betrayal. However, it must be pointed out that Newman was not always coherent in his ideas. He fought for freedom of expression especially in the university, and at the same time he wanted the church to exercise certain control over the institution. In *The Idea of a University*, in Discourse II, he asserts that there should not be any restriction on the range of university teaching, and in Discourse IX, he advocates a direct and active control by the church over Catholic university so as to avoid a rivalry between the two, especially in the area of theology. How to resolve this apparent conflict remains to be seen.

As seen earlier, Newman was ignorant of Asian religious traditions and cultures and spoke of China as 'a huge, stationary, unattractive, morose civilization'.[36] The huge impact he made on the religious and cultural life of England and the Oxford Movement was due to the fact that he was a child of his time. Some would doubt if he has something true and important to say to our modern world. After all, he was

35 *Apologia pro Vita Sua*,
    http://www.newmanreader.org/works/apologia65/chapter5.html, 252.
36 *The Idea of a University*,
    http://www.newmanreader.org/works/idea/article1.html, 252.

a Victorian gentleman, a member of a highly privileged class, and thus isolated from the great mass of his contemporaries.[37]

In spite of his genius, Newman had many failures in his life - the fact that secularism is so prevalent in western countries shows that his teachings hardly affect the modern world. There were people, both Catholics and Protestants, who thought his conversion to Roman Catholicism was insincere as it was made at a time when he was insecure and needed an infallible authority to give him assurance regarding his personal salvation. At Oxford University in the 1830s, he was actually a young bigot with a sense of intellectual superiority. In the 1860s, when there was fierce debate over science and religion, Newman thought the Protestants were in a mess, but Catholics were not – it was an illusion, of course.[38]

In 1851 Newman came to Ireland to be the rector of the Catholic University; he was rector until 1858. He felt a sense of failure because he believed he did not meet the objective of creating the intellectual headquarters for Catholics of the English-speaking world. Newman was made an editor of the *Rambler*, a liberal Catholic journal, but it lasted only two months (May-July, 1859). Another large enterprise, to which Cardinal Wiseman invited him, but later stopped him, was likewise a failure — the revision of the English Catholic Bible. And for twenty years, he was suspected by Rome, which misconstrued his teaching and his character. However, it is because of these failures, the struggles and anguish that he had to undergo to seek the truth, that Newman achieved his greatness.

As mentioned earlier, Ratzinger was very much influenced by Newman since his seminary days in Freising in 1946. He took from Newman his understanding of papal authority as a power that comes from revelation to complete natural conscience. It was under Gottlieb Soehngen (1892-1971), that Ratzinger studied Newman's *Grammar of*

---

37   See David Nicholls and Fergus Kerr, OP, 'Introduction,' 1-12 and 'Demythologising Newman,' 13-27, in *John Henry Newman, Reason, Rhetoric and Romanticism*, edited by David Nicholls and Fergus Kerr, OP (Carbondale: Southern Illinois University Press, 1991).

38   Owen Chadwick, *Newman* (Oxford: Oxford University Press, 1983), 74.

Assent. Soehngen had worked on sacramental theology and on the border issues between theology and philosophy, all of which are recurrent themes in Ratzinger's writings. Ratzinger regards Newman's teaching on the development of doctrine and the doctrine on conscience as decisive contribution to the renewal of theology. It is no wonder that as Pope, Ratzinger began his Apostolic Journey to the United Kingdom by beatifying Newman on 19 September 2010. Tracey Rowland said that that few English speakers seem to realize that Newman had a great influence on German Catholic thought in the first half of the twentieth century, and especially on the theology of Ratzinger.[39]

Newman was what the Irish poet, William Butler Yeats, would describe in 'The Statues': 'Born into that ancient sect. But thrown upon this filthy modern tide'. And it could be that the negative side of liberalism was sensed by Newman as a society where:

> Things fall apart; the centre cannot hold;
> Mere anarchy is loosed upon the world,
> The blood-dimmed tide is loosed, and everywhere
> The ceremony of innocence is drowned;
> The best lack all conviction, while the worst
> Are full of passionate intensity.[40]

Nonetheless, as we have seen, there is something of a liberal temper in Newman's writings. He was very much involved in the contemporary movement of thought. In spite of his anti-liberal polemic and rhetoric, Newman was a liberal spirit striving for the truth that would lead him out of the shadows and phantasm, as expressed in the motto he directed for his gravestone: *ex umbris et imaginibus in veritatem.*[41]

39   Tracy Rowland, 'The Influence of John Henry Newman on Benedict XVI', http://www.abc.net.au/religion/articles/2010/09/16/3013343.htm.

40   William Butler Yeats, 'The Second Coming,' http://ebooks.adelaide.edu.au/y/yeats/william_butler/y4c/part73.html.

41   From shadows and images into the Truth.

Bibliography

Alfeyev, Hilarion. Bp. 'European Christianity and the challenge of militant secularism'. *Ecumenical Review* 57, no. 1 (January 1, 2005): 82 – 91.

Allsopp, Michael E. and Ronald R. Burke, eds.. *John Henry Newman: Theology and Reform*. New York: Garland Publishing, Inc., 1992.

Aquinas, Thomas. *Summa Theologiae*. http://www.op.org/summa/

Balasuriya, Tissa. 'Some Asian questions on dictatorship of relativism'. *Voices from the Third World* 29, no. 1 (June 1, 2006): 14 – 31.

Bastable, James D. 'Newman's Judgment of Value in Liberal Education'. *Philosophical Studies* 31 (1986): 113 – 132.

Benedict XVI, Pope. 'The Church and the challenge of secularization'. *Christ to the World 53*, no. 5 (September 2008): 389 – 392.

Benedict XVI, Pope. 'Benedict XVI, Pope (2008-11-13) Healthy secularism for a peaceful coexistence'. *Osservatore Romano* (Weekly edition in English) 2070, (November 19, 2008): 6.

Berbusse, Edward J. 'Newman refutes contemporary liberal theologians'. *Homiletic and Pastoral Review* 84 (January 1984): 28 – 32.

Bertens, Johannes Willem. *The Idea of the Postmodern: A History*. New York: Routledge, 1995.

Boeve, Lieven and Gerard Mannion, eds. *The Ratzinger Reader*. London: T & T Clark, 2010.

Bowman, Jonathan. 'Extending Habermas and Ratzinger's *Dialectics of Secularization*: Eastern Discursive Influences on Faith and Reason in Postsecular Age', *Forum Philosophicum* 14 (2009):39 – 55.

Burrows, Mark S. 'A historical reconsideration of Newman and liberalism: Newman and Mivart on science and the church'. *Scottish Journal of Theology* 40, no. 3 (1987): 399 – 419.

Butler, Christopher. *Postmodernism: A Very Short Introduction*. Oxford: Oxford University Press, 2002.

Cameron, J M. 'Newman and Liberalism'. *Cross Currents* 30, no. 2 (Sum 1980): 153 – 166.

Chadwick, Owen. *The Secularization of the European Mind in the Nineteenth Century*. Cambridge: Cambridge University Press, 1975.

Chadwick, Owen. *Newman*. Oxford: Oxford University Press, 1983.

Chadwick, Owen. *From Bossuet to Newman*. Cambridge: Cambridge University Press, 1987.

Chaplin, Jonathan. 'Rejecting Neutrality, Respecting Diversity: From "Liberal Pluralism" to "Christian Pluralism".' *Christian Scholar's Review* 35, no. 2 (January 1, 2006): 143 – 175.

Chapman, Mark D. 'A Catholicism of the Word and a Catholicism of devotion: Pusey, Newman and the first Eirenicon'. *Zeitschrift für neuere Theologiegeschichte* 14, no. 2 (2007): 167 – 190.

Collins, Gregory. 'Clear Heads and Holy Hearts: The Religious and Theological Ideal of John Henry Newman'. *Irish Theological Quarterly* 60, no. 2 (1994): 156 – 157.

Coppa, Frank. *The Modern Papacy since 1789*. London: Longman,1998.

Cragg, G.R. *The Church and the Age of Reason 1648 – 1789*. Harmondsworth, Middlesex: Penguin Books, 1960.

Crosby, John F. 'Newman's witness against the spirit of liberalism in religion'. In *John Henry Newman*, 99 – 125. Rome: Urbaniana University Press, 1981.

Culler, A. Dwight. *The Imperial Intellect*. New Haven: Yale University Press, 1955.

Dallavalle, Nancy A. 'Cosmos and ecclesia: a response to Richard Lennan'. *Philosophy & Theology* 17, no. 1-2 (January 1, 2005): 279 – 291.

Daly, Gabriel. 'Newman, Divine Revelations, and the Catholic Modernists'. In *Newman and The Word*, edited by Terrence Merrigan and Ian T. Ker, 49-68. Louvain: Peeters Press, 2000.

D'Andrea, Thomas. *Tradition, Rationality, and Virtue*. Aldershot: Ashgate Publishing Limited, 2006.

Daniel-Rops, H. *The Church in an Age of Revolution*. London: J.M. Dent & Sons Ltd., 1965.

D'Costa, Gavin. *Theology and Religious Pluralism*. Oxford: Basil Blackwell, 1986.

D'Costa, Gavin. *John Hick's Theology of Religions*. Lanham: University Press of America, 1987.

D'Costa, Gavin. *The Meeting of Religions and the Trinity*. New York: Orbis Books, Maryknoll, 2000.

D'Costa, Gavin. *Theology in the Public Square*. Oxford: Blackwell Publishing, 2005.

D'Costa, Gavin. *Christianity and World Religions*. Oxford: Wiley-Blackwell, 2009.

De Lubac, Henri S.J. *The Drama of Atheist Humanism*. Cleveland: The World Publishing Company, 1963.

Denig, Stephen J. 'What would Newman Do? John Cardinal Newman and *Ex Corde Ecclesiae*'. *Catholic Education: A Journal of Inquiry and Practice* 8, no. 2 (December 2004): 162 – 174.

Dupré, Louis. *Religion and the Rise of Modern Culture*. Notre Dame, Indiana: University of Notre Dame Press, 2008.

Dupuis, Jacques S.J. *Toward A Christian Theology of Religious Pluralism*. New York: Orbis Book, 1997.

Eagleton, Terry. *The Illusion of Postmodernism*. Oxford: Blackwell Publishers, 1996.

Editorial. 'Newman's liberalism'. *Studies* 79 (Winter 1990): 341 – 342.

Ferguson, Thomas. 'The Enthralling Power: History and Heresy in John Henry Newman'. *Anglican Theological Review* 85, no. 4 (Fall 2003): 641 – 662.

Gellner, Ernest. *Postmodernism, Reason and Religion*. London: Routledge, 1992.

George, Francis E. 'How liberalism fails the Church : the Cardinal explains'. *Commonweal* 126, (November 19, 1999): 24 – 29.

George, Francis Eugene. '*Democracy and secularism*'. Origins 36, no. 44 (April 19, 2007): 709 – 717.

Glenn, Gary D. 'Is secularism the end of liberalism?: reflections on Europe's demographic decline drawing on Pope Benedict, Ha-

183

bermas, Nietzsche and Strauss'. *Catholic Social Science Review* 13, (2008): 91 – 116.

Groarke, Louis. 'What is Freedom? Why Christianity and Theoretical Liberalism cannot be Reconciled?' *Heythrop Journal XLVII* (2006): 257 – 274.

Gutting, Gary. *Pragmatic Liberalism and the Critique of Modernity.* Cambridge: Cambridge University Press, 1999.

Habermas, Jürgen and Joseph Ratzinger. *The Dialectics of Secularization.* San Francisco: Ignatius Press, 2006.

Hastings, Adrian. *The Theology of a Protestant Catholic.* Philadelphia: Trinity Press International, 1990.

Hastings, Adrian. *A History of English Christianity* 1920 – 1990. London: SCM Press, 1991.

Hauerwas, Stanley. 'Can Aristotle be a liberal: Nussbaum on luck'. *Soundings* 72, no. 4 (1989): 675 – 691.

Hedley, Douglas. 'Participation in the divine life: Coleridge, the vision of God and the thought of John Henry Newman'. In *From Oxford to the people*, 238 – 251. Leominster, Eng: Gracewing, 1996.

Heim, Maximilian Heinrich. *Joseph Ratzinger: Life in the Church and Living Theology.* San Francisco: Ignatius Press, 2007.

Hick, John and Paul F. Knitter, eds. *The Myth of Christian Uniqueness.* London: SCM Press Ltd: 1987.

Hick, John. *The Metaphor of God Incarnate.* London: SCM, 1993.

Holmes, J. Derek. 'J.H. Newman: History, Liberalism and the Dogmatic Principle'. *Philosophical Studies* 23 (1975): 86 – 106.

Hoppen, K Theodore. 'W G Ward and liberal Catholicism'. *Journal of Ecclesiastical History* 23, no. 4 (October 1972): 323 – 344.

Howsare, Rodney. 'Why begin with love? 'Eros, agape' and the problem of secularism'. *Communio* 33, no. 3 (Fall 2006): 423 – 448.

Hyman, Gavin. 'Postmodern theology and modern liberalism: reconsidering the relationship'. *Theology Today* 65, no. 4 (January 1, 2009): 462 – 474.

Jedin, Hubert, ed. *The Church in the Modern World.* New York: Crossroad, 1993.

Jenkins, Arthur Hilary. *John Henry Newman and Modernism*. Sigmar-ingendorf, Germany: Glock & Lutz, 1990.

Kenny, Terrence. *The Political Thought of John Henry Newman*. London: Longman, Green and Co., 1957.

Ker, Ian. *John Henry Newman* Oxford: Oxford University Press, 1988.

Ker, Ian. *The Achievement of John Henry Newman*. London: Harper-Collins Publisher, 1990.

Ker, Ian and Alan G. Hill, eds.. *Newman after a Hundred Years*. Oxford: Clarendon Press, 1990.

Ker, Ian. 'Newman on the Consensus Fidelium as "The Voice of the Infallible Church".' In *Newman and The Word*, edited by Terrence Merrigan and Ian Ker, 69 – 89. Louvain: Peeters Press, 2000.

Knitter, Paul F. 'Preface'. *The Myth of Christian Uniqueness*, edited by John Hick and Paul F. Knitter, vii-xii. London: SCM Press Ltd, 1987.

Küng, Hans and Julia Ching. *Christianity and Chinese Religions*. London: SCM Press, 1988.

Küng, Hans. *The Catholic Church*. New York: A Modern Library Chronicle Book, 2001.

Livingston, James C. *Modern Christian Thought*. New York: Macmillan Company, 1971.

Livingston, James C. *Modern Christian Thought*. New Jersey: Prentice Hall, 1997.

Luntley, Michael. *Reason, Truth and Self*. London: Routledge, 1995.

Lyotard, François. *The Postmodern Condition*. Manchester: Manchester University Press, 1984.

MacIntyre, Alasdair. *After Virtue*. Notre Dame: University of Notre Dame Press, 1984.

MacIntyre. Alasdair. *Whose Justice? Whose Rationality?* London: Gerald Duckworth & Co. Ltd., 1988.

MacIntyre, Alasdair. *Marxism & Christianity*. London: Gerald Duckworth & Co. Ltd., 1995.

MacIntyre, Alasdair. *God, Philosophy, Universities*. Lanham: A Sheed & Ward Book, 2009.

Martínez, Francisco Javier. "Beyond Secular Reason': Some Contemporary Challenges for the Life and Though of the Church'. *Communio: International Catholic Review* 31 (Winter 2004): 557 – 586.

McBrien, Richard P. *Catholicism*. New York: HarperCollins Publishers, 1994.

McCarthy, Timothy G. *The Catholic Tradition*. Chicago: Loyola University Press, 1994.

McGrath, Francis. *John Henry Newman: Universal Revelation*. Mulgrave, Victoria: John Garratt Publishing, 1977.

McLeod, Hugh, ed.. *European Religion in the Age of Great Cities, 1830 – 1930*. London: Routledge, 1995.

McLeod, Hugh. *Religion and the People of Western Europe*. Oxford: Oxford University Press, 1997.

McLeod, Hugh. *Secularisation in Western Europe, 1848 – 1914*. New York: St Martin Press, 2000.

McLeod, Hugh and Werner Ustorf, eds.. *The Decline of Christendom in Western Europe, 1750 – 2000*. Cambridge: University of Cambridge Press, 2003.

Merrigan, Terrence. 'Newman's Oriel experience: its significance for his life and thought'. *Bijdragen* 47, no. 2 (1986): 192 – 211.

Merrigan, Terrence. 'The Anthropology of Conversion: Newman and the Contemporary Theology of Religions'. In *Newman and Conversion*, edited by Ian Ker, 117 – 144. Edinburgh: T& T Clarke, 1997.

Merrigan, Terrence. 'Christianity and the Non-Christian Religions in the Light of the Theology of John Henry Newman'. *Irish Theological Quarterly* 68 (2003): 343 – 355.

Merrigan, Terrence. 'Newman and theological liberalism'. *Theological Studies* 66, no. 3 (September 2005): 605 – 621.

Milbank, John. 'Liberality vs. liberalism'. In *Evangelicals and Empire*, 93-103. Grand Rapids, Mich: Brazos Press, 2008.

Miller, Edward Jeremy. *John Henry Newman on the Idea of Church*. Shepherdstown, West Virginia: The Patmos Press, 1987.

Misner, Paul. 'The 'liberal' legacy of John Henry Newman'. In *Newman and the Modernists*, 3 – 24. Lanham, Md: University Press of America, 1985.

Moscovici, Claudia. *Double Dialectics*. Oxford: Rowman & Littlefield Publishers, Inc., 2002.

Murphy, Nancey. *Anglo-American Postmodernity*. Boulder, Colorado: Westview Press, 1997.

Murray, Donal. 'The secular versus religion?' *Origins* 37, no. 26 (December 6, 2007): 411 – 417.

Narveson, Jan and Susan Dimock, eds.. *Liberalism*. Dordrecht ; Boston: Kluwer Academic Publishers, 2000.

Natoli, Joseph and Johannes Willem Bertens, eds.. *Postmodernism: The Key Figures*. Malden, Mass.: Blackwell, 2002.

Nemoianu, Virgil. 'The Church and the secular establishment : a philosophical dialog between Joseph Ratzinger and Jürgen Habermas'. *Logos* 9, no. 2 (Spr 2006): 17 – 42.

Nemoianu, Virgil. *Postmodern & Cultural Identities*. Washington D.C.: The Catholic University of America Press, 2010.

Newman, John Henry. *Works of John Henry Newman*. Unless stated otherwise, all quotations with their paginations from the works of Newman are taken from this website: http://www.new mareader.org/works/index.html.

Nicholls, David. 'Gladstone, Newman and the politics of pluralism'. In *Newman and Gladstone*, 27 – 38. Dublin: Veritas Publications, 1978.

Nicholls, David and Fergus Kerr OP, eds.. *John Henry Newman, Reason, Rhetoric and Romanticism*. Carbondale: Southern Illinois University Press, 1991.

Nichols, Aidan. *The Thought of Pope Benedict XVI*. London: Burns & Oates, 2007.

Norman, Edward. *Roman Catholicism in England*. Oxford: Oxford University Press, 1985.

Novak, Michael. 'Remembering the secular age'. *First Things* no. 174 (June 1, 2007): 35 – 40.

Oakes, Edward T. 'Newman's Liberal Problem'. *First Thing*, no. 132 (April 2003): 43 – 50.

O'Connell, Marvin R. 'Newman and liberalism'. In *Newman today*, 79-93. San Francisco: Ignatius Press, 1989.

Pattison, Robert. *The Great Dissent*. Oxford: Oxford University Press, 1991.

Paskewich, J. Christopher. 'Liberalism Ex Nihilo: Joseph Ratzinger on Modern Secular Politics'. *Politics* 28, no. 3 (2008), 169 – 176.

Pelikan, Jaroslav. *The Christian Tradition Volume 5: Christian Doctrine and Modern Culture since 1700*. Chicago: The University of Chicago Press, 1989.

Quinn, John Raphael, Abp. 'Orthodoxy-as opposed to fundamentalism, theological liberalism, and integralism'. *New Oxford Review* 58 (May 1991): 15 – 23.

Ramachandra, Vinoth. 'Learning from modern European secularism: a view from the Third World church'. *European Journal of Theology* 12, no. 1 (January 1, 2003): 35 – 48.

Ratzinger, Joseph. *Church, Ecumenism and Politics*. New York: St Paul Publications, 1988.

Ratzinger, Joseph. *The Nature and Mission of Theology*. San Francisco: Ignatius Press, 1993.

Ratzinger, Joseph. *Truth and Tolerance*. San Francisco: Ignatius Press, 2003.

Ratzinger, Joseph. *Introduction to Christianity*. San Francisco: Ignatius Press, 2004.

Ratzinger, Joseph. *Christianity and the Crisis of Cultures*. San Francisco: Ignatius Press, 2005.

Ratzinger, Joseph, 'Cardinal Ratzinger's Homily'. Vatican Radio. http://storico.radiovaticana.org/en1/storico/200504/33987.html.

Ratzinger, Joseph. *Handing on the Faith in an Age of Disbelief*. San Francisco: Ignatius Press, 2006.

Ratzinger, Joseph and Marcell Pera. *Without Roots*. New York: Basic Books, 2007.

Rémond, René. *Religion and Society in Modern Europe*. Oxford: Blackwell Publishers Ltd, 1999.

Rhonheimer, Martin. 'Christian secularity, political ethics and the culture of human rights'. *Josephinum Journal of Theology* 16, no. 2 (Sum-Fall 2009): 320 – 338.

Roberts, Tyler T. 'Toward secular diaspora: relocating religion and politics'. In *Secularisms*, 283 – 307. Durham, NC: Duke University Press, 2008.

Rochelle, Jay C. 'Mystery and relationship as keys to the church's response to secularism'. *Currents in Theology and Mission* 19, no. 4 (August 1, 1992): 267 – 276.

Rorty, Richard. *An Ethics for Today: Finding Common Ground Between Philosophy and Religion.* New York: Columbia University Press, 2011.

Rosenberg, Randall S. 'Newman on the relationship between natural and revealed religion: his "University sermons" and the "Grammar of assent" '. *Newman Studies Journal* 4, no. 1 (Spr 2007): 55 – 68.

Rowland, Tracey. *Ratzinger's Faith.* Oxford: Oxford University Press, 2008.

Schwibach, Armin. "The 'new Enlightenment": how Benedict XVI is attempting to meet its challenge to faith'. *Inside the Vatican* 14, no. 5 (May 2006): 38 – 40.

Sharkey, Michael. 'Newman on the laity'. *Gregorianum* 68, no. 1-2 (1987): 339 – 346.

Sidenvall, Erik. *After Anti-Catholicism?* London: T&T Clark International, 2005.

Stout, Jeffrey. 'Homeward bound: MacIntyre on liberal society and the history of ethics'. *Journal of Religion* 69, no. 2 (April 1989): 220 – 232.

Strange, Roderick. *John Henry Newman: A Mind Alive.* London: Darton, Longman and Todd Ltd., 2008.

Taylor, Charles. *A Secular Age.* Cambridge, Massachusetts: The Belknap Press of Harvard University Press, 2007.

Therrien, Michel. 'John Paul II's use of the term 'neo-liberalism' in *Ecclesia in America*'. *Josephinum Journal of Theology* 8, no. 2 (Sum-Fall 2001): 130 – 142.

189

Thornton, John F. and Susan B. Varenne, eds.. *The Essential Pope Benedict XVI*. New York: HarperCollins Publishers, 2007.

Tillman, Mary Katherine.'Newman: the dialectic of "liberalism" and "conservatism"'. *Josephinum Journal of Theology* 9, no. 2 (Sum-Fall 2002): 181 – 195.

Torre, Joseph M de. 'Newman's struggle against the spirit of liberalism in religion'. *Homiletic and Pastoral Review* 106, no. 3 (December 2005): 44 – 47.

Tredway, J Thomas. 'Newman: patristics, liberalism and ecumenism'. *Christian Century* 82, no. 32 (August 11, 1965): 987 – 989.

Twomey, Vincent. 'When God is denied ...' *Inside the Vatican* 17, no. 8 (October 2009): 36 – 38.

Van der Bent, Ans Joachim. 'Christian and Marxist responses to the challenge of secularization and secularism'. *Journal of Ecumenical Studies* 15, no. 1 (December 1, 1978): 152 – 166.

Vargish, Thomas. *Newman: The Contemplation of Mind*. Oxford: Clarendon Press: 1970.

Vattimo, Gianni. *The Transparent Society*. Cambridge: Polity Press, 1992.

Vattimo, Gianni. *Belief.* Stanford, California: Stanford University Press, 1999.

Vattimo, Gianni. *After Christianity*. New York: Columbia, 2002.

Walgrave, J.H. *Newman The Theologian*. London: Geoffrey Chapman, 1960.

Walgrave, J.H., *John Henry Newman*. Rome: Urbaniana University Press, 1981.

Walsh, David. 'Newman on the secular need for religious education'. *Faith & Reason* 28, (1992): 359 – 385.

Weigel, George. *God's Choice*. New York: HarperCollins Publishers, 2005.

Williams, Rowan. *Arius*. London: SCM Press, 2001.

Wood, William D. 'Back to Christendom: one cardinal's response to secularism'. *Commonweal* 132, no. 12 (June 17, 2005): 8 – 9.

Wright, T.R. 'Newman on The Bible: A Via Media to Postmodernity'. In *Newman and the Word*, edited by Terrence Merrigan and Ian Ker, 211-249. Louvain: Peeters Press, 2000.

Yearley, Lee H. 'Newman's concrete specification of the distinction between Christianity and liberalism'. *Downside Review* 93, no. 310 (January 1975): 43 – 57.

Yearley, Lee H. *The Ideas of Newman*. University Park: The Pennsylvania State University Press, 1978.

Yeats, William Butler. 'The Second Coming'. http://ebooks.adelaide.edu.au/y/yeats/ william_butler/y4c/ part73.html.

Church Documents

Ad Gentes. On the Mission Activity of the Church. http://www.vatican.va/archive/hist_councils/ii_vatican_council/ documents/vat-ii_decree_19651207_ad-gentes_en.html.

Dialogue and Proclamation. Pontifical Council for Inter-Religious Dialogue. http://www.vatican.va/roman_curia/pontifical_councils/interelg /documents/rc_pc_interelg_doc_19051991_dialogue-and-proclamatio_en.html.

Gaudium et Spes. Pastoral Constitution of the Church in the Modern Word. http://www.vatican.va/archive/hist_councils/ii_vatican_council/ documents/vat-ii_cons_19651207_gaudium-et-spes_en.html#top.

John Paul II. *Redemptor Hominis.* http://www.vatican.va/holy_father/john_paul_ii/encyclicals/doc uments/hf_jp-ii_enc_04031979_redemptor-hominis_en.html.

John Paul II. *Redemptoris Missio.* http://www.vatican.va/edocs/ENG0219/__P7.HTM.

Lumen Gentium. Dogmatic Constitution on the Church. http://www.vatican.va/archive/hist_councils/ii_vatican_council/ documents/vat-ii_const_19641121_lumen-gentium_en.html.

Nostra Aetate. Declaration on the Relation of the Church to Non-Christian Religions.

Newspapers and Periodicals

ABC. Rowland, Tracey. 'The Influence of John Henry Newman on
   Benedict XVI'
   http://www.abc.net.au/religion/articles/2010/09/16/3013343.hm
The Christian Science Monitor.
   http://www.csmonitor.com/World/Europe/2010/1107/In-Spain-
   Pope-Benedict-XVI-lambasts-aggressive-secularism.
The Tablet.
   https://thetablet.co.uk/article/1866.
The Telegraph.
   http://www.telegraph.co.uk/news/newstopics/religion/the-pope/
   8006272/Pope-Benedict-XVI-warns-against-aggressive-
   secularism-in-Britain.html.